# THE DEATH OF LIBERAL DEMOCRACY?

*with best wishes*

*[signature]*

Joe Zammit-Lucia is an entrepreneur, investor, leadership advisor and commentator. He writes on business and politics for *The Huffington Post* (UK), *Het Financieele Dagblad* (Netherlands), *Die Achse Des Guten* (Germany), *The Guardian* (UK), *The Times of Malta* (Malta) and *The Stanford Review of Social Innovation* (USA). He is an investor and non-executive director in entrepreneurial ventures and advises senior business and institutional leaders on leadership in contemporary culture.

David Boyle is the author of a number of books including *The Tyranny of Numbers, Authenticity, Regicide* and *Scandal*. He is a former parliamentary candidate and editor of *Liberal Democrat News*. He is also policy director of Radix.

# The Death of Liberal Democracy?

Joe Zammit-Lucia and David Boyle

www.radix.org.uk

ISBN 978-0995503144

# Contents

# Foreword

**By the Rt. Hon. Tim Farron MP**

*Leader of the Liberal Democrats*

Everyone involved in Liberal politics in Britain and abroad knows the central paradox which lies at the heart of this timely book. We live in a society where liberal values are all-embracing. They are not everywhere, by any means, but they are the prevailing ideas which most of us live by – the right of everyone, whoever they are, to live out their full potential, however they see it themselves. Yet political parties dedicated to those values have been wrestling to put themselves at the heart of political debate.

It isn't clear why. But suddenly, because those liberal values are – if not in retreat – then under serious pressure and threat from the rise in nationalism, that question has become really urgent.

So I am delighted to introduce this book by Joe Zammit-Lucia and David Boyle, which provides us with a series of tentative answers to the question – and draw conclusions about future directions, and does so logically, trenchantly and with great style.

I don't agree with all of them. Some of their conclusions will challenge conventional Liberal thinking of recent decades. But I still want to give an enthusiastic welcome to their challenge, which is important, will lead I hope to debate – inside and outside Liberal parties – and may just be in the nick of time.

*Tim Farron*

# 1

# Introduction:
# The Liberal society and its enemies

*"The human race divides politically into those who want people to be controlled and those who have no such desire."*
**Robert Heinlein**

*"Our civilization... has not yet fully recovered from the shock of its birth - the transition from the tribal or 'closed society', with its submission to magical forces, to the 'open society' which sets free the critical powers of man."*
**Sir Karl Popper**

It is sometimes said that the Western world has become irreversibly Liberal, and that our Liberal democracies are firmly established. It is tempting to believe it. Liberal ideas – from the belief in freedom of the individual to gay marriage to open markets, free trade, open movement of people, the protection of property rights and the growth of largely secular, multi-cultural societies – have all become mainstream and, apparently, embedded in Western culture.

That is always a nervous proposition: the threats to that kind of Liberalism are obvious, even – perhaps especially – in Europe. But given that liberal ideas are mainstream and ascendant, we have to ask: does liberal democracy need to have political forces in Europe any more that are explicitly committed to Liberalism? Or is that need merely a delusion in the minds of congenital liberals? It is hard to find many people who would consider themselves to be 'illiberal', rather Liberalism is a question of meaning and degree.

All Western political parties and political philosophies hold embedded within them today values that are decidedly Liberal. Do such parties provide as much Liberalism as our societies want and are prepared to tolerate? Does this make those political forces that are explicitly Liberal either redundant or merely marginal – appealing only to a small proportion of the population that have a view of Liberalism that is disconnected from the views, values and concerns of the majority of the voting public? And does Liberalism as a primary philosophical and political platform provide the best route to addressing some of the key issues of the day – from terrorism to poverty and inequality and from the emerging problems of globalization to the excesses of *laissez-faire* market economics and secular economic stagnation? Or is Liberalism perceived as too soft and weak a political philosophy to tackle such difficult issues? These are the questions we address in this book.

Our focus in this book is political Liberalism rather than merely Liberal political parties. All political parties contain within them significant groups of people who would consider themselves to be Liberal in their political philosophy. We examine the evolution of Liberal parties as one indicator of political Liberalism but recognize that Liberal ideals are alive across the whole spectrum of political parties and hope that our suggestions may find some resonance with Liberals in whichever party they happen to live.

It is certainly true that much that is considered Liberal thought today permeates Western societies, but we argue in Chapter 1 that

- throughout the evolution of modern times - we have seen the old forms of tyranny that Liberalism was born to destroy replaced by different, and sometimes more subtle, forms of contemporary tyranny. These range from increasing government centralization, leading to a command and control social model, to the tyranny of technocracy, to the continued rise of the power of wealth and organized vested interests. Corporations, and especially large, multinational corporations, have become transformed from commercial and social entities to political institutions and, like trade unions and Non-Governmental Organizations (NGOs), they need to be considered as such.

Then there is the increasing impact of geopolitics and global trade on Liberal democracies, and here the threats are more obvious. On one side, terrorist organizations are increasingly waging a war to undermine Western Liberal democracy. Using violence and terror, they are successfully enticing politicians and security agencies to use the politics of fear to marginalize hard won freedoms in favour of arguable increases in security. On the other side, the perceived economic success of countries like China and Singapore is leading many to conclude that a little less Liberal democracy may be good for us all.

Finally, there is the changing perception of the desirability of free trade at a time when globalization becomes increasingly associated with the concentration of wealth and power among the few, rather than prosperity for the many. There has also been a progressive erosion of the identity and citizenship which makes Liberal democracy based on solidarity between individuals and groups impossible.

On the other hand, there is an emergent twenty-first century western culture that, albeit in different ways, seems more Liberal than what it replaced and provides huge opportunities for Liberals that can ride the new wave. The difficulty is that nineteenth and twentieth century Liberalism has very little resonance with this new culture. To remain relevant, Liberal parties need to draw on selected parts of their heritage, but at the same time they need to re-interpret Liberalism so that it is more relevant and more in tune with contemporary culture. As Paul Rabinow puts it in his book *Marking Time: On The Anthropology of the Contemporary*:

> "This position by no means rejects the use of older concepts; quite the contrary, but it does attempt to look at them anew, to refashion them in light of new elements and new problems."[1]

It is not clear that Liberals are achieving, or will be able to achieve, this change. This chapter makes the case, which is at the heart of this book, that the mainstream Liberalism we have grown up with in Europe is different from political Liberalism. We argue that this disconnect, and the failure of political Liberalism to renew itself, puts hard-won liberties at risk and risks rendering Liberals largely irrelevant in a twenty-first century political landscape.

To set the stage, we review in Chapter 2 where Liberalism came from, what it has achieved and how, in so many countries, Liberal parties are seeing an inexorable decline. We don't believe this decline is because Liberal thought is somehow redundant. But we do believe that it is due to a failure of most Liberals to re-invent themselves so that they can become once again what they once were – radical political forces with a coherent platform, at the cutting edge of political thought, focused on the core issues that matter to people. We argue that too many have reduced themselves to being cheerleaders for worthy but marginal causes and to trying to find some resting spot in the ever-vanishing middle ground between right and left. Or, as the authors of *The Orange Book* put it in the UK, becoming no more than "a philosophy of good intentions, bobbing about unanchored in the muddled middle of British politics".[2]

Some Liberals have forgotten that radicalism used to be the defining characteristic of Liberal politics and, steeped in a deadening political correctness, have instead decided to compete for the title of most unexciting parties in the political landscape. Others argue that Liberalism has abandoned its traditional roots, yet neither are they making any attempt to forge a coherent, contemporary political philosophy. They are becoming instead a 'bulging and messy repository' that makes Liberalism a moving target with an orthodoxy that shifts with every new intellectual fashion. Paul Gottfried, in his book *After Liberalism,* argues that coherent Liberal philosophy has been replaced by an aggregate of issues that happen to be in vogue at any particular time such as gay rights, radical feminism, environmentalism and unrestricted immigration. [3]

He argues that the term 'Liberal' has been 'decontextualized' and "means whatever the user wishes it to signify provided he can browbeat others into accepting his definition". He also argues that, contrary to the founding principles of Liberalism, many Liberals today have bought into the idea of the managerial state "as an arbiter of victimological claims".

Our interest in this book is to explore ways in which the West can stop and reverse what seems to us a slide into a post-Liberal era. If that can be achieved, it is not clear to us whether it will be led by political parties that explicitly position themselves as Liberal or whether it will fall to mainstream parties of the centre-right and the centre-left to maintain Liberal ideals. It is quite possible that some explicitly Liberal parties will simply fade away as they fail to find relevant differentiation within the political spectrum or as they continue to place Liberal philosophy ahead of Liberal politics. In other words, much like Jeremy Corbyn's socialism, they continue to place purity of ideology and a tedious but relentless focus on their own hobby horses ahead of the pursuit of political power. Some don't even have the ambition or the self-belief to achieve political power. In that case it will fall to others to ensure the survival and revival of Liberal politics within their own, broader, political philosophies.

Whoever ends up being the standard bearers, we believe that a revival of Liberal politics can only be based on the development of a clear and coherent political philosophy that, in the best Liberal traditions, is bold, radical, contemporary, and resonant with the public. It needs to be a radical platform that, rather than lazily splitting the difference between Right and Left, actually repudiates that dying dichotomy. This would need to start with a deep understanding of those emerging elements of contemporary culture that provide a strong foundation on which a refreshed Liberal politics can be built.

This understanding is not to be discovered through opinion polls, though, they will have a role. Instead, it requires a deeper understanding of the currents and counter-currents that are shaping attitudes and beliefs as we move from the discipline and organized so-called 'rational' thought of the modern to the much more complex, more fluid, faster moving and less easily codified attitudes of the contemporary.

We review our perception of these changes in Chapter 3, where we attempt to draw an impressionistic picture of where, in cultural terms, we have come from and where it looks like we might be going. We also argue that that there is a further dichotomy that needs to be actively repudiated – the one between private and public sectors – the divide that depends on old-fashioned ideas of Right and Left.

In *Capitalism 4.0*, Anatole Kaletsky argues for a future that rejects the ridiculous notions that, depending on one's political colour, either the public sector or the private sector is the only one that holds the key to progress. Both have a different and complementary role in building prosperity and society. He contends that "Strong government and strong markets are both necessary for the successful functioning of the capitalist system." We need both to be highly effective and we need to re-define what collaboration between public and private sectors should come to mean in the twenty-first century.[4]

That kind of future is not to be found in the Public-Private Partnership model that successive governments have embraced in the UK, with its limited focus on finance, procurement and public service delivery. Instead, we catch glimpses of it in the Estonian model that has delivered, steadily and over a twenty-year period, what is arguably the most advanced digital economy in the world through full integration of private and public sector efforts. It is possible to discern emerging new Liberalisms in other parts of the world, just as you can see them in corners of UK life, public and private.

Finally, we argue that Liberal politics has forgotten its fundamental roots – a radicalism that pushed progress by being opposed to the status quo and that was focused on breaking down the oppressive power of the establishment. In the UK, the Liberal Party lost its turn of the century dominance when it gave up on its reformist, Liberalizing credentials and, after decades in power, itself became part of the Establishment. It died opposing the Suffragette movement, the Irish independence movement and the emerging workers' movement – all movements that were fundamentally Liberal, but seen as upsetting to the comfortable status quo (though it presided over reforms to all three). The Establishment has always tended to be on the wrong side of history, and that is what has always made Liberalizing movements successful.

Yet, throughout Europe, Liberals now want to see themselves as part of that establishment – serious administrations in waiting. They believe that this somehow makes them seem more 'grown up' and 'serious' – an attitude that is more reflective of the self-image of the parties' leadership than it is of true Liberal instincts. It is therefore no surprise that radicalism is today more readily associated with new insurgent parties like Italy's Five Star Movement than it is with supposed Liberals.

Some Liberal parties talk glibly about being the 'challengers', yet they are structured and behave just like every other political party, timidly putting out the same statements and bland, sanitized press releases that are as meaningless as they are useless. As such, they no longer deserve the moniker of being Liberal and, failing a dramatic change in attitude, they are condemned to continue their inexorable decline.

### The open society

What does all this mean for a new Liberal politics?

Let's start with Stalingrad. If you read Anthony Beevor's classic account of the battle, the overwhelming impression is one of senseless waste. Two vainglorious dictators, who insist on taking every decision – and who are immune to human feelings of compassion for the men under their direction – simply waste their men in blood and suffering. It is a terrifying vision of the sheer inefficiency of dictatorship. While it was taking place, the Viennese philosopher Karl Popper, a refugee from the Nazis, was working on the political implications of his philosophy of science.

How could you prove anything inductively, given that – no matter how many times the sun rose in the morning – it was no proof that it would do so again? Popper came up with an interim answer to the problem David Hume had set two centuries before: you may not be able to prove what you believe about the world, no matter how often an observation or experiment takes place, but you can *disprove* it.

Popper used the example of swans. It doesn't matter how many white swans you see, it still doesn't prove that all swans are white. But if you see a black swan, then you *know* they are not.

Popper's home city was in the hands of totalitarians, and he quickly found himself applying this insight to politics too. In doing so, he produced one of the classic twentieth century statements of philosophical Liberalism, *The Open Society and its Enemies*. He said societies, governments, bureaucracies and companies work best when the beliefs and maxims of those at the top can be challenged and disproved by those below. That is how societies learn fastest: closed systems discourage learning – openness encourages it.

Popper was flying at the time in the face of the accepted opinions of the chattering classes. They may not have liked the totalitarian regimes of Hitler or Stalin, but people widely believed the rhetoric that they were somehow more efficient than the corrupt and timid democracies, as our own elite believe now.

Not a bit of it. Real progress required "setting free the critical powers of man", he said. The possibility of Popper's challenge from below – in what he called 'open societies' – is the one guarantee of good and effective government or management. Those human beings at the front line, those most affected by policy, will always know better about their own lives or their own work than those at the top. The more open you are to them, the flatter the hierarchy, the more the critical information will be available to learn and move forward. It is, in its own way, the antidote to Stalingrad.

Popper provided the best explanation why Liberalism works and why, in practice, we need to devolve power down as far as possible through society. Because that is the way we develop, have ideas: it is the justification for a flatter society, and an effective, more equal economy too – because we can't waste the talent that otherwise moulders away unused.

Liberals spread power, not because it is nice – nor because it has an electoral appeal (though it does) – but because open societies can change and develop, and closed societies can't. Hierarchical, centralized systems, by their very nature, prevent that critical challenge from below.

In this book, we take Popper as a starting point. We argue that, today, we find ourselves in societies that are dominated by centralized, unmanageably large institutions, controlled by a powerful elite that still believes it has all the answers and is able to engineer the world to its own model of perfection. Such institutions – being both state and non-state actors – impose their will and inevitably create large, centralized, bureaucracies that stifle opportunities for experimentation and, therefore, of pragmatic progress. Popper calls for 'piecemeal social engineers,' a term that is maybe reflected in today's emerging generation of social entrepreneurs.

We argue that Popper's sense of an open society represents a solid foundation on which a new Liberal politics can be built. In later chapters, we apply this model to the economy, finance and business, to health and public services, to the environment, to our educational system, to technology and to Europe as a politico-cultural construct. We envision a society that is fundamentally Liberal in the sense that it liberates people from the tyranny of technocracy and of centrally controlled institutions, in order to unleash their creative powers. A belief that those human beings at the front line, those most affected by policy, will always know better about their own lives or their own work than those at the top. The more open you are to them, the flatter the hierarchy, the more the critical information will be available to learn and move forward.

This kind of open approach leads to small, piecemeal improvements that add up to a more flexible, more adaptable, more effective whole. In our view, this approach meshes with many of the elements that we see emerging in contemporary culture. Of course, that kind of approach requires a degree of political leadership that is in short supply. The pursuit of small improvements based on decentralized experimentation will lead to differences across geographies and communities. These risk making politicians vulnerable to criticism that some are getting a better deal than others. Yet we believe that such criticism will die away once people realize that governments are giving people more control of their own future and, rather than micro-managing them, they are providing them with the tools and opportunities to decide their own priorities and create their own vision of the future – and shaping new institutions that help them do so.

We also argue that a Liberal society must be founded on a Liberal economy. Liberals have to understand, just as their founding parents did, that the economy must be front and centre of any Liberal political programme that is to have any chance of success. Typical Liberal concerns such as civil rights, minority rights, environmental protection, and so on are undoubtedly important, but they can't create a Liberal society without an economic model that is itself fundamentally Liberal.

## Power

Any political model has to have a coherent theory of power – something which many Liberals have traditionally been uncomfortable with – even in how they run their own internal party affairs, never mind the country.

'The purpose of getting power is to be able to give it away.' If we've heard this once, we've heard it a million times from those who see themselves as Liberals. This highly Liberal quote is attributed to Aneurin Bevan, the Welsh Labour politician who was never part of any Liberal party. This can be seen as ironic, given that socialism at the time was about concentrating power and ownership in the hands of the state but it vindicates our earlier contention that Liberal ideals are not the exclusive property of Liberal parties. That said, while some of the sentiment of the Bevan statement is undoubtedly correct, it is far from complete.

An open society gives people the space to imagine the world differently and allows them to find ways to create or contribute to the changes necessary to bring about the changes they want. But giving people this sense of their own power also, paradoxically, requires a determined exercise of power. Power abhors a vacuum.

A government that strips itself of power and authority invites other groups to fill that vacuum and assume power in its stead. We have seen this repeatedly throughout human history and we are seeing it again today.

To go further, a functioning society is not possible without a government that is able to exercise power meaningfully and effectively. In his article *Weak States, Poor Countries*, Nobel Prize winning economist Angus Deaton argues that one only has to look at the poverty, deprivation and civil wars that plague those countries that have ineffective, powerless governments to realize that an effective, powerful state is an essential component of a functioning society.[5]

The difference between Liberalism and other political philosophies lies in how a Liberal state chooses to exercise its power. In *Freedom's Power*, Paul Starr argues:

"The core principles of Liberalism provide not only a theory of freedom, equality, and the public good, but also a discipline of power—the means of creating power as well as controlling it."[6]

Where Liberalism differs from other political philosophies is that it exercises its power to control power rather than to exercise total control over individuals or to make them dependent on the state. Liberalism has, throughout history, also used power to break down the elite's hold on power – something that is anathema both to conservatives and to socialists, who differ mainly in which type of elite they believe should hold power.

Liberals go further than others because they don't accept equality of opportunity merely as a theoretical construct. They focus on equality of *achievable* opportunity. The conservative approach that argues that everyone starts with the same opportunities, and expects them to fight it out in the marketplace in a Hobbesian war of all against all, is just as unacceptable to Liberals as the socialist race-to-the-bottom search for bland uniformity.

For Liberals, equality of opportunity is insufficient. Liberals are about breaking down the considerable barriers to achieving those opportunities. And that involves the wielding of major power against the powerful vested interests that stifle challenge from below.

Finally, one of the fundamental tenets of Liberal democracy is that democracy derives its legitimacy, and therefore its power, from a politically engaged population not from the ruling class. Politicians tend to define the amount of power they feel they have by the number of seats they hold in their respective parliaments. Such political power is undoubtedly important, crucial even. But when this conception of power becomes degraded into a narrow focus on electioneering, it turns into a myopic and misguided idea that leads – and indeed has led – to ever decreasing political engagement by the voting public and, ironically, ever decreasing effective power for elected politicians.

Liberals used to be revolutionaries, and revolutionaries have always understood that political power comes first from the power of ideas powerfully expressed. Ideas that inspire and resonate emotionally with the public. Ideas that are expressed powerfully enough to get the voting public to be politically engaged. Ideas that foster public trust in a new political establishment. Ideas that can credibly be implemented.

And, just as an aside, that is why we use Liberal and Liberalism throughout this book rather than that other currently fashionable political term 'progressive'. Liberal is a word that, well used, has emotional power. Progressive is the preferred term of the more bureaucratically minded, politically correct set that would rather strip terms of any emotion as they prioritize inoffensiveness over emotional engagement – a politically disastrous attitude.

All this implies that Liberals must do more to re-interpret the meaning of their traditional *laissez-faire* attitude to government. Liberals must strive to maintain a government that is powerful enough to prevent other groups from monopolizing power for their own interest and, by doing so, provide a more even distribution of power. This is hardly the natural state of affairs, as history demonstrates.

But it also implies something else. It suggests that political parties need, above all else, to present the world with challenging and coherent ideas. And they need to do so powerfully and emotionally. Without that, no amount of campaigning and no amount of counting of votes will allow them to thrive. As the Scottish proverb puts it: you don't make sheep any fatter by weighing them.

## Citizenship

In Chapter 3, we address some of the issues related to identity politics. This may be one of the more difficult areas for Liberal thought. We define citizenship as a sense of belonging to a particular community and carrying both the rights and the obligations that arise from belonging. Globalization, free movement of people and the threats to the nation state as a cohesive political and social unit, the overwhelming power of a detached technocracy – all these factors are undermining people's sense of citizenship. Yet without such a shared sense of citizenship, a Liberal democracy based on shared norms, the rule of law and solidarity with others becomes impossible to sustain.

Liberals have traditionally presented themselves as internationalist, as supporters of the free movement of people and of multiculturalism. But they have, so far, failed to have any coherent response to the impact of these political positions when they undermine a sense of citizenship and, consequently, destabilize Liberal democracy itself.

A counter-current arises from the way that an over-powerful, technocratic state also undermines a sense of citizenship. Towards the end of the twentieth century, the focus on individual rights was often at the expense of individuals' sense of responsibility to their communities (however defined). While Bismarck set up a system of universal health care to unify the nation, our benefits system is no longer underpinned by a strong sense of citizenship, but presented as a question of individual rights and an exercise in compassion. That undermines unity. When Gottfried suggested that "Democratic citizenship has come to mean eligibility for social services and welfare benefits", that is what he meant.[7]

This sentiment has inevitably led to, and also been driven by, today's brand of retail politics where parties compete with giveaways to favoured voting groups. John Kennedy's inaugural address included the injunction: "Ask not what your country can do for you — ask what you can do for your country". This is not the kind of language that political parties use now, which means they are obscuring the realities: ask not what the NHS can do for you, ask what you can do for the NHS – suggests a more active citizenship. It also has the virtue of explaining a vital balance that is now missing. Instead political parties have reduced themselves from entities with a clear moral purpose to being election-winning machines. This was foreseen as a major problem associated with an electoral democracy. Sean Wilentz, in *The Rise of American Democracy*, notes that James Madison worried that "the arts of electioneering would poison the very fountains of liberty."[8] The challenge we face today is for parties to re-discover how moral purpose, rather than electoral venality, can be converted into electoral success – and how electoral success can be converted to power that is used for the common interest rather than narrow party interests.

## Liberalism refreshed

Benito Mussolini was not a Liberal. He said that "the Liberal state is a mask behind which there is no face; it is a scaffolding behind which there is no building." The challenges of a rapidly changing world poses the risk that this is indeed how the electorate is coming to view Liberal politics everywhere. As a result, we are seeing the revival of political strongmen in countries that, we all thought, had strong, well-established democratic credentials. This is a reaction to the increasingly obvious failure of *laissez-faire* taken to extremes.

Our aim in this book is to try to put forward some ideas that may be useful as Liberals of whichever party continue to construct the building behind Mussolini's scaffolding, and to replace what some consider naïve positions with pragmatic and effective ones that earn the confidence of the electorate. We don't pretend to have answers to all the varied and difficult questions facing political Liberalism today. Our aim is instead to present some ideas that might stimulate others to imagine what such a building might look like.

We believe that to be able to stand tall, such a building will have to be a distinctively twenty-first century edifice. It will need to be functional, cohesive and sturdy. But more than that, it needs to have some kind of soul. It must move people emotionally. It needs to be more than just a building, but an identity that is visibly different from the buildings constructed by the parties of the Right and the Left – and not some bland average of the two. And, while it needs to reproduce the solidity and integrity of the grand Victorian edifices of the past, it cannot merely ape or reproduce them, but rather must be appropriately shaped and constructed to reflect our evolving contemporary culture. Above all it needs to be human not technocratic, because if technocracy has any overwhelming skill, it is its ability to stifle any kind of emotion and to kill any form of desire for engagement.

It isn't our aim here to develop detailed, country-specific policy ideas – policy development is a second order issue that can only flow from a clear overarching vision. What we hope is to start a discussion about the overall framework within which such policies can eventually be developed. Most importantly, we would like to stimulate debate about what a twenty-first century Liberalism should stand for and what meaning voters should be encouraged to make of political Liberalism.

A very significant proportion of Europeans, maybe the overwhelming majority, have strong Liberal tendencies. Yet Liberal parties in Europe are in progressive decline. As we hinted earlier, we believe that this decline of Liberal parties across the continent doesn't represent a 'declining market' for Liberal politics. It actually represents a failure of Liberals to capitalize on these inherent Liberal values, to bring them up to date and to apply them to people's lives. Our hope is that this book might make a modest contribution to the revival of political Liberalism in

Europe and that it might provide some food for thought and some encouragement for Liberals – whichever political parties they happen to be aligned with – to continue to carry forward the flame for truly Liberal democracies.

We conclude this introduction with a statement from Robert Kennedy that could serve as a useful reminder of what Liberals have always been about: *"There are those who look at things the way they are, and ask why. I dream of things that never were, and ask why not."*

# 2

# The near death of Liberalism

*"The most important characteristic of economic policy is its
centrality in the political process."*
**Sir Samuel Brittan, *The Politics of Economic Policy***


Magna Carta Libertatum.

This seminal document is now eight centuries years old. Lord
Denning described it as "the greatest constitutional document of
all times – the foundation of the freedom of the individual against
the arbitrary authority of the despot". As made clear by its full title,
it is a fundamentally Liberal document. Lord Denning's
description captures the essence of Liberalism – an essence that
remains as true today as it has developed since the thirteenth
century.

But the human struggle for Liberalism pre-dates the Magna
Carta by several centuries. The Ancient Greeks, whose society was
divided into slaves and freemen, believed that freemen should have
a 'liberal' education. By this they meant an education that
encouraged freedom of thought and resistance to indoctrination –
an education that encouraged people to understand their rights
and obligations as citizens.

The struggle for liberation from tyranny has been a long and
often violent one. The Glorious Revolution, the American
Revolution, the French Revolution, the Russian Revolution and

many others are all products of Liberal thought as so clearly and emotively expressed in Delacroix's iconic painting representing the February Revolution and titled 'Liberty Leading the People'.

As we outlined previously in the case of the Suffragette and workers' movements, the struggle for liberation has also had to take on and, eventually, overthrow political elites that described themselves as Liberal. Because once Liberal forces tend to end up defending the status quo once they fail to understand, let alone adapt to, the ways in which people continue to re-define the meaning of liberty and pursue its new forms.

The long history of the struggle for liberation teaches us important lessons. The first is that the overthrow of power itself requires organised power. The second is that entrenched interests will defend their privilege, sometimes to the death. And finally, that the road to Liberalism is never smooth and it is never ending. On that road, one form of tyranny is often, at least in the short term, simply replaced by another form of tyranny – be it the Reign of Terror post-French Revolution, the tyranny of Soviet style communism, or the chaos and repressive regimes that have emerged following the Arab Spring.

Also, as we have seen in Chapter 1, there are other, more subtle forms of technocratic tyranny that now flourish in democratic states. The drive to accumulate and concentrate power seems to be a basic human instinct – one that will make sure that Liberalism will always have a job to do. That means that those who are truly liberal should always have an important role to play in the political playing field.

## Political Liberalism
Liberalism as a strand of philosophical thought and, later, as a

political movement is a relatively recent development. It has its origins in the eighteenth century Age of Enlightenment. Liberal thinking flourished in the British, French and American enlightenment movements of the eighteenth and nineteenth centuries. John Locke is credited with founding Liberalism as a distinct philosophy with the then radical notion that government required the consent of the people.

Philosophically and politically, Liberalism was the product of an intellectual class. It rode the wave of enlightenment optimism, the belief in science and reason as instruments of progress and the belief that every person had the right to life, liberty and property. It burst into the nineteenth century on the crest of a scientific wave.

It is, therefore, no coincidence that the first Liberal Party, formed in the UK, emerged the same year as the publication of Charles Darwin's *The Origin of Species*, just five months apart. Both were the product of the same mid-Victorian scientific optimism, though neither were fully formed ideologies at this stage. Using science and reason, both were revolutionary, overthrowing the embedded notions of the political, scientific and religious establishments. The original meeting to form the new party, held in Willis's Rooms in St James Street in London, included well over two hundred Whigs, Radicals, Peelite Conservatives and pioneer Liberals like John Bright – testament to the fact that Liberalism knows no party boundaries. When Lord Palmerston helped Lord John Russell up onto the platform, there was a huge burst of cheering.

*It's the economy, stupid*
It was particularly clear to the founders that the primary tools with

which a Liberal society could be built had to be economic. Well before Bill Clinton's now famous dictum about the economy, it was clear to the founders that a Liberal society could only be achieved by crafting a Liberal economy. The two went together.

Nor is the insight that Liberal societies can only ever be products of a Liberal economy particularly new. On a visit to the Museum of the Acropolis in Athens, we came across this informational sign:

> "Athens in archaic period found itself in obscurity through social upheaval from unequal wealth distribution. Son instituted important measures which provided relief to poor farmers, cancelled the debts which had led them into a form of slavery, restricted the power of the aristocracy and granted political rights to a much broader range of the population. This laid the foundations of economic development but was too moderate and balanced to be sufficient. Peistratos threw out the aristocracy through tyrannical rule and trade and the arts flourished."

As we shall see later, this undeniable relationship, between politics and economics, seems to have been lost in many Liberal circles today, where the focus on civil liberties, minority rights, education and other typical Liberal concerns has led to a loss of the bigger picture and the fundamental point that, in the modern as in the ancient world, it is the structure of the economy that will determine whether a society is Liberal or otherwise.

The founders of the new Liberal Party put political economics at the centre of their programme. They built on the economic insights of Adam Smith and the classical economists. Their ideological inspiration was partly free trade, which they understood as the new frontier of the campaign to abolish slavery, believing that protectionism kept people poor and threatened world peace by locking the poorest into economic relationships that benefited the rich. They were also, to some extent, influenced by John Stuart Mill's philosophy, a Liberal and more humane version of utilitarianism, forged partly by Mill's father's relationship with Jeremy Bentham, partly by his own long affair with the pioneer feminist Harriet Taylor and partly his own nervous breakdown as a young man, which led him to doubt his father's puritanical ideological edifice.

Economically, the new Liberals believed that freedom from excessive government intervention was an essential component of liberty. This led to a philosophy of *laissez-faire*, market driven economics – maybe an appropriate response to the many limitations to the functioning of markets in the Victorian era. Yet the fundamental issue that was never tackled was the contradiction inherent in the combination of *laissez-faire* with wielding the power that is necessary to break down vested interests. The process of repealing the Corn Laws earlier in the century had clearly shown the struggles involved in breaking down the power of landowners, then the most politically powerful group. The intellectual conflict between *laissez-faire* and the wielding of political power continues to plague Liberals of all parties to this day.

*Utopian optimism*
Darwin was working on the proofs of his book in 1859. Mill's own work, *On Liberty*, was published the same year as the meeting, earlier in the year. The Chartists were on the wane, the year of

revolutions a decade before, and the Great Exhibition eight years before, cast forward their rival shadows of pessimism and optimism. The new Liberal Party, formed that year on 6 June, was to be history's chosen instrument to put this optimism into policy and to bring it to bear on the life of the nation.

The new party was bound up with the idea of enlightened human progress – human evolution in its broadest sense. This is how one of the first Liberal MPs saw it, Darwin's great propagandist Sir John Lubbock, writing in his own book *Prehistoric Times* six years later:

"It is surely unreasonable to suppose that a process that has been going on for so many thousand years should have now suddenly ceased... The future happiness of our race, which poets hardly ventured to hope for, science boldly predicts. Utopia, which we have long looked upon as synonymous with an evident impossibility, which we have ungratefully regarded as 'too good to be true', turns out on the contrary to be the necessary consequence of natural laws, and once more we find that the simple truth exceeds the most brilliant flights of the imagination."[9]

There is the optimism of Liberalism, confident of its scientific support and its destiny, and with its own ability to evolve built in, so to speak.

Many Liberals still maintain some kind of utopian vision as an important part of their worldview. But the world has changed significantly since those times and it is debatable how credible and effective such unbridled optimism can be in a world that is much more complex and much more cynical than it used to be, and where people's belief that political parties of any colour can deliver positive change has largely unravelled. The utopian vision is also one that appeals primarily to a certain educated, intellectual class. Today, it carries the risk of coming across to the more practically minded as a mush of unrealistic good intentions while reflecting a lack of empathy and understanding of the realities and struggles of life at the bottom of the heap.

What does hold them together is that Liberals rely on an optimistic vision of the future, but – as we shall see – their main role in the twentieth century has been as political sceptics to totalitarian or scientific utopias. That remains an absolutely vital role for Liberals now.

Both Liberal philosophy and Liberal politics have evolved with the times since the founding of the first Liberal Party. But this change cannot be described as a cohesive evolution of a Liberal political philosophy. The concept of Liberalism necessarily creates a broad church. Many buy into its fundamental tenets. The challenges arise when those broad tenets start to be translated into a cohesive philosophical standpoint, a coherent political platform, and then a set of practical policies. Here, individual interpretations start to diverge.

The creation of a practical and cohesive platform is made more difficult by the open-minded acceptance of many different views that many have come to believe to be inherent in any grouping that calls itself Liberal. But such a view fails to distinguish between Liberalism as a philosophical set of concepts and Liberalism as a political platform. The two are far from being the same thing. When political Liberalism degenerates into nothing more than an all-encompassing philosophy of any idea that can be called Liberal, it fails to be politically relevant or remain politically effective. What many Liberals don't grasp is that failure to make a clear distinction between Liberal thought, and the necessity to develop a much more cogent, effective and therefore necessarily more focused Liberal politics, makes them politically ineffective. It undermines their own ability to build Liberal economies and liberal societies.

This is perhaps best encapsulated in G. K. Chesterton's comment: "As much as I ever did, more than I ever did, I believe in Liberalism. But there was a rosy time of innocence when I believed in Liberals."[10]

The evolution of Liberal parties reflects these difficulties. Parties evolved by growing to take in varied groups that shared the broad ideals of Liberalism, only to be subject to the formation of factions with different philosophies, many of which eventually break away over disagreement over the overarching political platform of the time. This is maybe best summed up in the opening sentence on Liberalism in the *Stanford Encyclopaedia of Philosophy*: "As soon as one examines it, 'Liberalism' fractures into a variety of types and competing visions."

It is this repeated process of accretion and fracture that has characterised the evolution of liberal politics. A process that was made more difficult by a new conflict that arose – that between *laissez-faire* and the emerging philosophy of social intervention.

That division has fed into the decline of Liberalism as a political philosophy. Liberalism was the instrument that forced UK governments to reform and by which Europe created the institutions it needed to avoid war, however inadequate they are now. Liberalism around the world has driven in different directions since then – in the USA it means 'social democrat'; in Germany it means free market. Liberalism has become so broad that it has subsumed them both. Liberalism has driven the tolerance to people's sexuality and religion, just as it lay behind the equality between the sexes. And its very success led to its difficulties. People came to take it for granted – the days when it was an Italian word for liberation had gone; it looked very general rather than specific. It looked almost like a *lack* of conviction, rather than a precise political philosophy. It looked like relativism, or postmodern cynicism – as if nothing mattered very much – except that what really mattered to Liberals was not what mattered to most of the population.

*Social Liberalism*
In the UK, Joseph Chamberlain's radical integration of municipal ambition and agrarian reform shifted Liberalism into a more social agenda. The Newcastle Liberals in the 1890s, and their intellectual backers in Oxford, adapted Liberalism to the understanding that poverty was part of the tyranny that they had been formed to tackle. People could not be free if they were poor. This exacerbated the political crisis inside the Liberal Party and ultimately led to the split from Chamberlain and his followers, together with the Whigs and critics of Home Rule for Ireland.

The loss of Joseph Chamberlain's radicalism may have been inevitable, given the clash between his growing ambitions and Gladstone's leadership, and also perhaps because of the emerging clash over the nature of free trade that would come to dominate that political generation. It famously divided the Conservative Party so fundamentally that one of Arthur Balfour's lieutenants described himself as "nailing his colours firmly to the fence".

There were intellectual advantages for the influence of Fabian thinking on Liberalism. It led to the People's Budget in 1909 and the dawn of old age pensions. It led to a deeper understanding of the meaning of liberty, and a new practical expertise in the development of local government.

But it also lost other people along the way. The Distributists, the non-Fabian economic critique by former Liberals Hilaire Belloc and G. K. Chesterton, left to form the Distributist League in the 1920s, though their thinking was adapted by Jo Grimond's leading policy influencer, Elliott Dodds. The failure to adapt and renew Liberalism cost key names to both right and left in the 1930s through to the 1950s. Then a breakaway group, primarily Liberals, left the party in the 1970s to form the Ecology Party, which became the Greens.

None of these losses were important in terms of people, but they were hugely important because of the loss of those strands of thinking inside mainstream political Liberalism.

## The failures of Liberalism in the late twentieth century

If there is a 'Distributist wing' of the UK Liberal Party, or the Lib Dems later, then it isn't a label that is either used or understood much, except by academics. But, whatever we call it, there has remained a developing strand inside political Liberalism that has become hugely important towards the end of the twentieth century, injecting ideas around community development, the environment and human scale.

These are occasionally taken up in other parts of the political spectrum, but – because they are no longer seen as mainstream – they have struggled to be embedded in mainstream debate or policy. The tradition became exemplified by a man who would not have described himself as a Liberal, the economist E. F. Schumacher, author of *Small is Beautiful*. Yet it was Schumacher who borrowed the Roman Catholic doctrine of *subsidiarity* –

which had been developed so strongly by Belloc and the Distributists, and which was adopted (at least in theory if not so well in actual practice) by the European Union to explain the importance of decisions being taken at the appropriate level in the hierarchy.

This concern for issues around human scale, which academics might describe as Distributist, has remained a potent force in Liberalism during the twentieth century. It gave the party its beard and sandals image of the 1970s (everyone has beards and sandals now). It led to its reputation for flaky new approaches – a by-product of taking directions away from the establishment view: "As usual, the Liberals have produced another set of sound and original ideas," quipped Conservative prime minister Harold Macmillan before the 1959 general election. "Unfortunately, none of the sound ideas are very original and none of the original ideas are very sound."

But where this intellectual tradition paid off for the UK Liberal Party was under Jo Grimond's leadership from 1956. The reward was the first signs of what became a Liberal Revival. It was the anti-Fabian critique of Keynesian economics, linked with a scepticism about technocratic progress, launched as much as anything else by the Liberal economist Friedrich Hayek in his hugely successful book *The Road to Serfdom*, echoing some of the themes of Belloc's *The Servile State* from three decades before.[11]

Pointing to Hayek as the father of the Liberal Revival seems strange today when he is much reviled in Liberal circles as the father of neoliberalism, a creed with only passing, perverse links to Liberalism. But that is to misunderstand his important role in launching the shift towards self-determination that followed the Second World War, a time of overwhelming scepticism about conventional progress and official utopias. It was also overwhelmingly Liberal.

It meant that, under Grimond's leadership, the Liberal Party then became the unfocused and uncrowned political wing of the voluntary sector, the voice of the critique of conventional 'progress' by conservationists, housing campaigners, radical architects and environmentalists. It became, in the fullness of time, the instrument by which the toxic and constipated world of UK local government was turned upside down. What Hayek launched, and others too – like Borsodi in the USA and Schumacher in the UK – was a challenge to accepted progress, just as it was a challenge to conventional categories. That generation broke away from official progress, rejecting the idea that the government would decide where to funnel resources, and launched a whole series of movements that rejected the Spirit of '45, along with big bureaucracies, official instructions, closed shops, concrete jungles, high rise flats – anything that treated individuals as amorphous groups.

The result has been the roller-coaster ride we have all travelled during our lifetime – the end of deference, the beat generation, the Liberal Revival, the voluntary sector, gender and sexual equality, Shelter, and the breakdown of simple class divisions, the green movement, and so on... These have not always been Distributist causes, it is true, but they derive from a Distributist scepticism about progress. If Distributism was a conviction that both capitalism and socialism inevitably ended in tyranny, the Liberal revival involved a scepticism about any official-ism which trapped individuals in categories. It wasn't the same, but one derived from the other and both derived from Liberalism.

So when, in the second half of the twentieth century, a new

radical generation emerged that disputed collective utopias – and the whole idea of 'progress' as conventionally understood – it left the mainstream struggling, as they still are today. Slum clearance was intended as a solution to urban squalor – and Labour Housing Minister Richard Crossman had urged the complete demolition of Oldham – but it replaced tight-knit communities with new alienating slums. The new towns programme, finally abandoned by Labour's Environment Secretary Peter Shore in 1976, had failed to halt the degradation of the inner cities. Dividing traffic from pedestrians – the idea in Colin Buchanan's ground-breaking report *Traffic in Towns* – had relegated pedestrians to risky concrete passages. Atoms for Peace – the polite alternative to nuclear bombs – had led to a blind alley of high-level nuclear waste. Conventional progress led by a well-meaning intellectual elite was not working.

And there was a resurgent Liberal Party under Grimond ready to give political voice to this critique, and by the 1970s to oppose the nuclear energy programme. There was no mention of the environment in the Liberal manifestos under Grimond, but the critique of modernity was there when Liberal strategist and historian Roger Fulford asked the way in Harlow New Town: "To my embarrassment she told me, through her tears, 'I simply hate it here.' A Ruskin was needed to do justice to the contrast between the kind hearts of the planners and the true wishes of mortal man."[12]

The reference to Ruskin was a hint. This was more evidence of a revival of the Liberal Party's Distributist tradition. Yet those who voted Margaret Thatcher to power in 1979 were people in the grip of Hayek's original ideas, but also those in search of a sense of independence who were in the grip of his spirit. In fact, the

Thatcher government enacted one of the few pieces of genuinely Distributist legislation the establishment has ever dared to do – the sale of council houses at huge discounts to their tenants.

Unfortunately, the policy was brought into disrepute by two factors. The first was the failure to replace the houses with new ones. The second was the electoral underpinnings of the policy. First of all it was implemented in the belief that, in turning more of the nation into home owners, more voters were likely to identify with conservative rather than socialist principles. Secondly, it was not really designed to make people freer: it was designed to keep the new home owners shackled to their debts, so that they would think twice before going on strike or undertaking any other disruptive action that would threaten their regular income.

What made this interesting politically was that the mainstream Left could not understand it. The socialism which emerged in the UK in the 1930s was intelligent and sophisticated, thanks to the guidance of George Orwell. But even Orwell had a horror of 'alternative' or 'cranky' opinions, like those that would emerge from the green movement. "If only the sandals and the pistachio-coloured shirts could be put in a pile and burnt," he wrote, "and every vegetarian, teetotaller, and creeping Jesus sent home to Welwyn Garden City to do his yoga exercises quietly."[13]

It wasn't that *The Road to Wigan Pier* was somehow blind to these issues. Quite the reverse: Orwell's description of the woman poking a stick up a dirty drain, with "the most desolate, hopeless expression I have ever seen", is as evocative as any modern environmentalist writer. But for Orwell, the Welwyn rant was an invocation against crankery, and those counter-cultural issues which emerged from Liberalism in the 1940s and 50s got up his nose.

There is the history of late twentieth century British Liberalism in a nutshell – derided by the mainstream Left, but helping to articulate the most powerful social movements dedicated to self-determination, and yet confused themselves. And it was confusing for anyone still in the grip of the Fabian mindset – self-determination launched on the world by free market economists, and articulating issues about women or the environment that seemed to have no place at Westminster.

Unfortunately, thanks to those who waited in the wings, on both sides of the Atlantic, Hayek's neoliberalism turned out to be wholly illiberal. It shored up the status quo, rather than undermined it. It became an apologia for monopoly rather than a critique of it. Instead of a manifesto for challenge from below, it became a justification for protecting the strong and wealthy. And in direct contravention of Hayek's purpose, neoliberalism emerged, not as a critique of pseudo-science, but yet another pseudo-science itself.

One of the tragedies for Liberalism was also that parliamentary politics increasingly sidelined this strand of its Distributist tradition. It was, for example, one of the long-term effects of the merger with the SDP. The Distributist tradition still lives on in the Liberal Democrats, but it is less understood, less articulated, more an object of suspicion inside the party as well as outside it. It was the loss of the Distributist wing, this Liberal concern with human scale, which has led to the three major failures of the political creed towards the end of the twentieth century, with serious consequences for our lives.

First, it meant that political Liberalism in the UK began to lose touch with the roots of the Liberal Revival. The huge movement which Hayek had launched, rather unwittingly – rejecting scientific socialism and deeply sceptical about conventional progress – was set free to splinter into its various parts, the housing association movement, the voluntary sector, the feminist movement, the green movement, forgetting perhaps that at their roots these movements of self-determination had sprung from postwar Liberalism. It meant that political Liberalism had to struggle to express itself as a coherent force. Liberalism forgot the purpose of community politics – the most potent expression of this strand in conventional political terms – and wondered why its support tended to waft away. It is a political tragedy for the politics of self-determination: there was a time when it was becoming a coherent political force. It isn't any longer.

Second, the loss of Distributism meant that there was no intellectual force capable of holding together the two wings of Liberalism – the social and the economic. Both became intellectually stuck, unable to learn from each other, forgetting that one was simply the expression of the other in a different field. It meant, in particular, that economic Liberalism became stolen by American economists with a very different agenda. When Milton Friedman re-wrote *The Road to Serfdom* for an American audience (*Capitalism and Freedom*, 1962), it was no longer Liberal. But by then, Liberals had lost touch with this element of their make-up and were unable to provide a coherent critique.

Which brings us to the third failure. Friedman redirected neoliberalism by denying that monopoly was a problem. This flew in the face of British Liberalism just as it flew in the face of American Liberalism. It was partly the result of the suicide of Friedman's teacher, the great Liberal economist Henry Simons, in 1946. But it was also the result of a failure of political Liberalism to articulate any response. The political force which had tackled monopoly on both sides of the Atlantic, as the core purpose of Liberal free trade – rather than just the licence for the rich and powerful to do what they liked – had gone silent on the subject.

We are still living with the consequences of that great error.

## Where now?

Across Europe since then, Liberals have had their successes, as radical groups like D66 in the Netherlands, or the free trade Liberals in Germany's FDP, pushed the European Liberals back and forth. Non-Liberal centre parties have emerged and disappeared in France and Spain without articulating a more modernised version of the Liberal agenda. In the UK, the Liberal Democrats, a politically uncomfortable combination of free market Liberals and social democrats, rose to form the backbone of the Liberal group in the European parliament and then fell away again.

But they have been hamstrung intellectually by their failure to understand the tradition they represent, and the powerful role they have played – explicitly but also unwittingly – in the last half century. Liberals are also embedded in political parties of all colours. But they too struggle to put forward a coherent Liberal politics inside the big tents of the major parties. Periodically their politics finds itself in the ascendancy, only to fall back again as socialists and conservatives pull these parties back to their original roots, either for fear of losing their appeal to the core base or in response to short term events.

A broad-minded acceptance of any group or set of ideas that might conceivably fit into some definition of Liberalism has, as we have seen, been a characteristic of Liberal politics almost since inception. It has had important consequences. Prime among them is, as we outlined earlier, the failure to identify and develop, over time, a cohesive Liberal political platform. This has meant that Liberalism across Europe has lacked the intellectual tools to adapt their political critique of the new and emerging tyrannies that were forging new manacles for the people of Europe. It has meant that Liberalism has not been able to resist the assumption by the new technocrats that they should simply assume the powers of elected politicians. Nor have they been able to defend the institutions of democracy while services were shackled into ineffective units by the new utilitarians. In other words, by being too open, Liberalism has left itself without a unifying political platform, a coherent direction and a clear identity. All this is vitally important because, lacking a cohesive political identity, Liberals are, and will remain, unable to bring about the change that our societies need.

It is this dilemma that faces Liberals now. How have they managed to create this social revolution in self-determination, in the feminist movement and the movement for sexual and race equality, and yet everywhere they still struggle to articulate their purpose?

The answer, we suggest here, is that Liberalism has forgotten the full breadth of its tradition. It has allowed social Liberalism to get divorced from political Liberalism – as if the highest purpose of mankind was to serve on a committee. It has lost touch with the purpose of Liberalism, corroded by postmodern cynicism, or by fear of the spiritual in politics – and the spiritual was a vital element in Liberalism before.

Most of all it has divorced social and economic Liberalism, so that the two appear to be in separate universes. And, as we have outlined above, a Liberal world relies on an injection of Liberalism into economics. You cannot separate the two, because they drive each other. As a result, mainstream Liberalism has drunk at the river of forgetfulness about economics. They knew they used to know something about it, but now they barely see it – it is like an estranged partner they can't bear to meet.

If we are going to give Liberalism back its driver, we need to heal that division, so that this particular political philosophy – so vital to our future – can fire on both cylinders again.

# 3

# The evolution of culture

*"I have often reflected that the causes of the successes or failures*
*or men depend upon their manner of suiting their conduct*
*to the times."*
**Niccolo Machiavelli**

This Machiavellian insight is as relevant today as it was in the fifteenth century, or before. We have seen so far that political movements rise rapidly to greatness because they are able to capture the spirit of the times. They fall just as rapidly because they cling on to the beliefs that led to their rise, while remaining blind to the cultural changes that have overtaken them – however significant those changes might have been. Liberalism today suffers the same weakness. As Barbara Tuchman puts it in *The March of Folly: From Troy to Vietnam*: "Mental standstill or stagnation – the maintenance intact by rulers and policy-makers of the ideas they started with – is fertile ground for folly."[14]

If we are to witness a Liberal Revival, Liberals must adapt their politics to the culture of the times. In this section, we therefore attempt to provide a picture of contemporary culture. Because culture is not static and any one cultural period is a largely artificial definition that contains strong elements of all that went before, we will draw our picture by meandering through Western cultural evolution over a period of time starting around the sixteenth century. Our picture will, of course, be brief and highly limited. It will have more in common with an Impressionist or Cubist painting than with the detailed representation of a Canaletto. Finally, we draw some conclusions of what contemporary culture means for some of the key questions that political liberalism has to address.

Culture is a vague, amorphous and nebulous construct. It manifests itself in the pleasures, hopes and struggles of everyday lives. It is revealed in the narratives and stories of the anthropologist; in literature and the arts; in Twitter feeds and Facebook posts; but not in the stylised models of the economist, the financier or the central banker – detached as they are from human realities. Many avoid the subject because it doesn't lend itself to study in the structured and reductive form of the modern. You can't measure culture and put it on a spreadsheet. Therefore, for some, it is best ignored. Yet it is the fundamental underpinning of people's behaviours, their values and their political beliefs. In our meander, we will aim to tell a story. Where have we come from? Where are we now? Where might we be headed?

## The legacy of enlightenment

"I think therefore I am."

This Cartesian statement may, more than any other, define the culture of the Enlightenment. Starting in the sixteenth or seventeenth centuries, the Enlightenment ushered in what we have come to know as the Age of Reason. Descartes' statement is a synthesis of the Enlightenment idea that knowledge and reason – the ability to think and to act rationally – represent the most important human characteristic, that it separates the human from the animal. Enlightenment thinking is a European product. It produced, over a period of some two hundred years a cultural revolution that came to spread from Europe to dominate much of Western thinking and, through colonialism, much of the globe.

The Enlightenment began with a scientific revolution. The rise of the natural sciences combined with philosophical 'rationality' was to become the way of explaining the world and the authoritative guide to practical life. Science, knowledge and rationality would, henceforth, be the basis of human progress while religion, the previously dominant spectacles through which meaning was constructed, slowly started to become marginalized as superstition. Tradition was no longer seen as something to be revered, but rather as its own form of superstition, which merely served to hinder human progress. The importance of knowledge, as then defined, as the driving force for human progress, is maybe best exemplified by the fact that the most influential publication of the Enlightenment was the *Encyclopédie*, a twenty-eight volume repository of knowledge and Enlightenment thinking compiled by a team of 150 scientists and philosophers.

It does not take much to see how Enlightenment thinking disturbed the pre-enlightenment world order. Science and reason substituted religion and the divine right of monarchs as the source of all legitimate authority. It is also clear why, despite the revolutions that followed, Enlightenment thinking simply ended up transferring power from one group of elites to another – from monarchs and the church to scientists and intellectuals.

Liberal thinking is a child of the Enlightenment. Reason, science and empiricism where, as we have outlined earlier, born as the twin sibling of Liberalism with its focus on liberty and tolerance. They were the tools that Enlightenment thinking would use to undermine and, eventually, overthrow the authority of the hegemonic union of church and state. John Locke's *Second Treatise of Government* (1690) is the classical source of modern Liberal political theory. Locke argued that everyone exists naturally in a state of freedom, that, as regards power, "no one having more than another" and "being all equal and independent, no one ought to harm another in his life, health, liberty, or possessions."[15]

Through much evolution in detail and interpretations, the basic tenets of Liberalism have remained largely unchanged. They continue to reflect fundamental Enlightenment thinking and, maybe more importantly, their appeal today remains strongest among an educated, intellectual class.

Enlightenment thinking underpins the origins of Liberalism – a philosophy based on optimism, a positive view of mankind and a belief that rational thought, empiricism and scientific knowledge form the appropriate bases for human progress – a philosophy that casts to one side any other claims to political legitimacy – be that birthright, religion, nation, tribe, gender or many of a myriad other claims to power.

The trouble was that the optimism of Enlightenment was soon put to the test, and in its very birthplace – France. And it was found wanting.

The French Revolution was, perhaps, the best political reflection of the Enlightenment and Liberal ideals of individual freedom and equality. The institutions that were not based on these ideals were violently overthrown. But then what? As the revolutionaries attempted to replace the previous 'divine' order with rational, secular institutions, they failed. Eventually they had to revert to violence and terror in order to control and govern the people. "The devolution of the French Revolution into the Reign of

Terror is perceived by many as proving the emptiness and hypocrisy of Enlightenment reason," says the Stanford Encyclopaedia, "and is one of the main factors which account for the end of the Enlightenment as an historical period."[16]

This turn of events illustrates a couple of points that we shall explore in more detail later, but which will be central to the task of re-defining Liberalism now. The first is that critical thinking can end up being better at finding reasons to tear existing institutions down than to find ways of building new and more effective ones. The second, and maybe more important one, is that rationality has no moral content. Moral judgments are more emotional than rational and a society that deifies science and rationality to the exclusion of all else risks descending into a state of amorality, and a consequent loss of any form of social cohesion.

This may be best illustrated by the developments of the Renaissance, one early manifestation of the period of Enlightenment. The Renaissance, an important prequel to the Enlightenment, has been described as "the period when the values of this world replaced those of the hereafter." As a result the 'civilized' world lost its moral compass and the Renaissance became part of an era of worldly human progress as well as great moral failure.

The six Renaissance Popes epitomized this shift. They devoted themselves and their institution to worldly pleasures, the accumulation of wealth and patronage of the arts, forgetting totally that their primary mission was supposed to be a moral one. The result was total failure and the breaking apart of Christendom with the Protestant secession. Some may see parallels to today's world where many see the relentless pursuit of economic growth as the primary political goal while any kind of moral judgments are frowned upon. The Enlightenment was the period where science and reason won out over morality and emotion. It laid the path for the journey to the Modern. It is along this path that we will continue our cultural meander.

## The age of modernity

What we will describe as the Age of Modernity probably represents one of the most dynamic and fast paced eras of human development to date. It contains much complexity and spans a long period of time.

The cultural bed on which the Enlightenment took root and flourished was based on a belief in the power and capacity of human beings, a desire for discovery through science and knowledge and the start of the idea of freedom of thought, enabled by valuing humanity, literacy and education.

Modernity is maybe not as much a period as a way of thinking, and in a sense we have been 'moderns' for two centuries or so, adapting the Enlightenment into the modern world of the twentieth century. Enabled by political and cultural acceptance, the evolution of science and technology gave us what we might consider today to be the modern world. A greater scientific understanding of the natural world and developments in technological ability gave us the industrial revolution, urbanization, and increased movement of goods, capital, information and people, eventually evolving into the phenomenon of globalization. Science and technology combined with an evolving capitalist economic structure to bring great benefits to humanity – benefits that are obvious to us all but far too numerous to capture here.

Social organization also changed dramatically. The growing

belief in our ability to 'manage' everything around us led to the development of bureaucracies that were tasked with organizing our lives from local services to whole empires. 'Management' became classed as 'a science' and its combination with our belief in the value of information and knowledge led to what has been described as the modern obsession with 'evidence' to underpin every action. The collection of data as evidence burgeoned and no opinion was worth anything unless underpinned by figures.

As societies became more complex, and the body of knowledge started to grow exponentially, specialization came to be more and more highly valued. This was coupled with the increasing primacy of science and its status in modern society. As a result, no specialist discipline was considered credible unless it followed scientific methods. Sociologists morphed into social scientists, the study of politics turned into political science and naturalists became natural scientists. Disciplines like economics also felt the necessity to become more 'scientific', adopting some of the methods of the natural sciences – much to the rage of some of the German sociologists. By the twentieth century, there was no longer room for the polymath – the Renaissance Man or Woman. This was the era of the expert, someone who is valued for knowing more and more about less and less.

Politically, developments were just as rapid. The march of the Liberal ideals of the Enlightenment continued. Secularization, freedom of the individual and equality of citizenship evolved into widely acknowledged concepts. But turning them into reality was a slow process that required the painstaking and often violent breakdown of the power of established ruling elites. Women did not get the vote anywhere until the late nineteenth century; workers did not get significant rights until the mid-twentieth;

slavery was not declared illegal globally until 1948 (and remains alive today in practice); segregation was not abolished in the United States until 1964; Apartheid did not end in South Africa until the 1990s and the last colony did not disappear until the dawn of the twenty-first century.

The modern era also saw the rise of the nation state as the primary political entity. The evolution of the nation state allowed the building of social cohesion through a sense of national identity and the modernization of societies through the spread of universal education, mass literacy, broadening of health care availability and the application of a uniform rule of law.

## The challenges of modernity

There is little doubt that, whatever historical span one would like to include under that moniker, modernity has delivered huge improvements to human existence against almost any metric one would choose to measure it. But it also brought with it a number of side effects and characteristics that are now posing cultural, political and social challenges. We will examine these challenges briefly for two reasons. First, they are the challenges that political parties of all colours have to face and respond to. Secondly, they give us an insight as to why, with all the benefits that have accrued, we have chosen to start evolving beyond the ideas of modernity to move to what some have called the 'postmodern'.

'Management' is probably the single word that captures both the benefits and the downfall of modernity. Advances in what we can manage and how has, during the modern era, narrowed our vision of how we judge the success of any initiative. In a scientific, 'evidence-based', modern culture, success is judged by efficiency and measurable outcome. While this is not to be dismissed out of hand, this narrowing of thought has led to many issues.

Philosophically, this approach has developed in step with utilitarianism, which tried to evaluate the moral acceptability of any course of action by its outcome. Any initiative is moral if it produces the greatest good for the greatest number – with "good" progressively becoming defined almost exclusively in terms of accumulated wealth. The classical utilitarians like Jeremy Bentham and John Stuart Mill were also founders of modern Liberal thought. In this sense, at least, utilitarianism is inextricably linked with modern Liberalism. Such consequentialism, where actions are judged by their collective outcomes, fit naturally into the modern era of rationality and the use of scientific evidence and they created a very specific social view of what constituted progress – a view that became identified with Liberal thought and which persists very widely today.

The main problem with this approach is that it eliminates any form of moral judgment except through an evaluation of consequences. In practice, for example, moral questions like whether torture or mass surveillance are acceptable become reduced to whether the information gathered in this way improves national security or not – a discussion we have seen played out at length in the wake of the behaviour of US forces in Iraq and the post-Snowden debate on national security. The question of whether torture or widespread surveillance of innocent citizens are morally acceptable irrespective of outcome becomes marginalized. Similarly, in *A History of the American People*, the historian Paul Johnson takes the position that the use of nuclear weapons in Hiroshima and Nagasaki was justified because it brought the Second World War to a more rapid end and thereby probably saved more lives.[17] A utilitarian argument that does not even begin to stimulate a discussion about whether the use of nuclear weapons against a civilian population, and without any nuclear threat to oneself, is ever morally justified.

Utilitarianism flourishes in a world that sees itself as 'rational' and appeals to those who see themselves as rational beings. Consequences are things that can be rationally argued for and can be evaluated and measured. This philosophy inexorably led to the modern approach of evaluating all policy and other initiatives on the basis of economic cost-benefit analyses. Policy is set on the basis of economic models that project the greatest measurable good (only economic good, mind you) – an approach that is presented as perfectly rational and technocratic (determined by 'experts') and therefore the best guide to policy.

While such utilitarian approaches clearly have their place, it has become clear that they are insufficient and, if taken to excess, can lead societies down some highly undesirable paths. While the Siamese twins of reason and consequentialism are not to be abandoned, they are not sufficient to be a guide to policy, because they all too easily lead us to a place where ends justify means. Slavoj Žižek warns of such in his book *First as Tragedy, Then as Farce,* where he interprets Hegel's Cunning of Reason as potentially making "even the vilest crimes instruments of progress."[18]

The horrors of an unbridled rationality and of a modernity perverted and taken to excess were brought into sharp focus during a visit to the museum in Berlin dedicated to the terror of the SS. The Nazis took the idea of society as engineered, 'managed' machine, abandoned any kind of moral judgment and threw out the democratic accountability that would hold back 'progress.' They set about constructing what would, from their perspective, be the perfect modern society. Their dream was built on the search for human and ideological perfection achieved through technological means. Never before had we seen in such sharp focus the realities of utter dehumanization, moral bankruptcy and the reduction of individuals to irrelevance in the hyper-modern machine. We need to think of Nazi Germany as a terrifying caricature of modernity, rationality and utilitarianism gone out of hand.

Yet if we argue that consequentialism is an important but insufficient moral compass, we will need an alternative. In such cases, one has to resort to other moral frameworks be they religious, cultural or based on societies' moral intuitions. For Rational Man, this is an uncomfortable place to be as it whips the carpet of rationality from under our feet, forcing us to recognize other forms of moral judgment that go against most of what secular, scientific modernity stands for. Liberals are caught in this dilemma probably more than any other political grouping.

While the horrors of Nazi Germany were, thankfully, an aberration, the adverse effects of modernity started to be felt acutely in the twentieth century. It was during this period that we saw that the rational society perfectly planned by the experts had substantial flaws.

First it led, in many countries, to the centralization of power to make sure only the best experts guide the development of our societies and our economies, a version of Frederick Winslow Taylor's 'One Best Way' of scientific management. Those at the helm knew best what everybody wanted and how we should all lead our lives – and they could plan for it all to happen, manage it efficiently and evaluate the outcomes against defined metrics. The Soviet Union was, of course, the most extreme example of this mentality, but the same undercurrent plagues us all to this day.

From the supposedly efficient high rise developments that turned slums into worse slums to the perfectly planned new towns that ended up being unloved and unwanted. Or the cities blighted by a modernist architecture that was efficient and perfectly rational while lacking any kind of human appeal. Or 'evidence-based' health care decisions that are taken centrally by committee based on generic cost benefit analyses, without any consideration of local conditions or the needs of individual patients.

Modernity has brought great progress. It has liberated the marginalized and the enslaved and spread prosperity across much of the globe. As always, new ideas and new cultures work well until they are taken to extreme. It is only in the last several decades that the limitations of the modern are becoming apparent. These arise from the modern's uncritical lionization of knowledge and rationality over human values and the consequent rise of a meritocratic society that has ended up replacing one ruling class with another while undermining concepts of solidarity.

But maybe its biggest failure has been the inability to replace effectively the moral compass that was previously provided by organized religion with any other commonly accepted form of moral judgment. To the critically observant, these failings of the modern have been obvious for some time. Jonathan Swift wrote *Gulliver's Travels* in 1726. Gulliver reported how the Lilliputians chose people to occupy public office: "They have more regard for good morals than for great abilities, for, since government is necessary to mankind, they believe ... that Providence never intended to make management of publick affairs a mystery, to be comprehended only by a few persons of sublime genius, of which there are seldom three born in an age."[19]

## The modernization of politics

Politics too, has become modern. While, for a period, this brought with it great benefits in terms of better decisions being taken by better informed politicians, here too the trend may have run its course. For many decades, many have urged the political class to become more 'business like'. It is not clear, however, what that means. One interpretation is that politics should become more rational, more evidence based and generally more efficiently run. In other words more modern. Again, it is hard to quibble with that as long as one bears in mind that politics is not a business and therefore cannot be run using the same basic principles of a business. Politics is about making choices that, as we have outlined, are largely moral, ethical and values based – something that tends to become lost in a modern world where politics gets reduced to a managerial process focused on winning elections, and this is in turn driven by a consequentialist philosophy that any policy is a good policy only if it wins more votes than it loses.

As Colin Crouch puts it in his book *Post-Democracy,* this reduces politicians to "something more resembling shopkeepers than rulers, anxiously seeking to discover what their 'customers' want in order to stay in business."[20]

If we accept that politics is primarily about making moral and ethical choices – and finding pragmatic ways to implement those choices – rather than simply about rational and efficient management, then we might find in modernity an explanation for the decline of politics. Recent neuroimaging and behavioural studies have shown that the activation of those neural networks associated with analytical reasoning leads to the actual suppression of brain activity associated with social, emotional and moral cognitive processes. In other words, the more we use and develop the rational parts of our brains, the less we are able to use the empathic part and to make abstract moral judgments.

As politics becomes more focused on the rational, it therefore loses its ability to deliver its primary purpose – that of making moral judgments. In such a world, politics risks becoming redundant. Political parties will all gravitate towards the same 'rational' agenda making any differences between them largely irrelevant. We might therefore just as well leave it all to technocrats and managers. Which, as we outlined in Chapter 1, is exactly where modernity has led us.

Modernity will not end suddenly. Its way of thinking will continue to be pervasive and drive much of politics, policy-making and other walks of life. But modernity is also past its peak. Its fundamental philosophies have started their slow decline and will be replaced by a new, emerging cultural milieu that will continue to evolve through the twenty-first century and beyond. If Liberalism is to be re-born, it will have to emancipate itself from its intellectual roots in the Enlightenment and the modern, re-interpret its fundamental tenets without abandoning them, and march in tune with, and possibly lead, the new twenty-first century cultural developments just like it led those of previous periods.

But to get there we need to have some understanding of what the new cultural milieu might look like.

## The Age of Unreason?

"We live in an Age of Unreason. I am used to making rational, evidence-based decisions. But these days everyone has an opinion and every opinion seems to be equally valid. We have people being whipped up by populist politicians and others with narrow agendas and it seems impossible to have reasoned arguments any longer."

These words came from a senior Liberal politician who, comfortable with the rationality of the modern, has started to feel its decline in his bones and wondered what chaos was in store. To a greater or lesser extent, many of us feel the ongoing cultural change, are not fully able to make sense of it and are worried or frustrated, or both, by the decline of the old order. Here we argue that we are not, in fact, entering an age of unreason. Rather we are evolving beyond the modern to a new era that will bring its own benefits and disadvantages but that is, in fact, more Liberal and provides great opportunities for Liberals who can ride the new wave.

What we describe here is a web of interweaving developments that are having an impact on contemporary ways of thinking, contemporary culture and people's expectations. The processes we describe are not all new. Some of the concepts and ways of seeing were articulated centuries ago. But technological, political and social developments have come together to give life to new ways of thinking and new ways of being. The last couple of decades or so have provided added impetus to this cultural change through the development of the digitally interconnected society.

None of the developments we describe here stands alone. Everything is interconnected. Our separation of the discussion into different sections, while essential to give some sort of structure, needs to be recognized as somewhat artificial. But we hope that we can create a sense of the cultural and political implications of today's fast moving, urban, techno-driven, cyber-linked, unstructured, freewheeling, postmodern society.

## Authority

There was a time when a letter to a major newspaper signed by a couple of dozen of the great and the good – with a few Nobel Prize-winners thrown in for effect – would get people's attention and be listened to with some respect; maybe even acted upon. Today, it is more likely to initiate a storm of disagreement and often ridicule in the blogosphere.

The past response represents the culture of the modern – where there was only one 'truth' to which the elite held the key. In today's culture, where ideas and information flow freely and where, thankfully, we have seen a general rise in prosperity, level of education, health and longevity, there is an emerging confidence among the general population in their ability to challenge imposed truths. The information age powered by digital technology has enabled and hugely accelerated a massive cultural transformation, a democratization of ideas that have led people everywhere to empathize with Nietzsche's perspective that: "All things are subject to interpretation. Whichever interpretation prevails at a given time is a function of power and not truth."

We shall return to the question of power later in this chapter. But in this current context, we ask: what were the sources of authority that previously determined what we all believed and that now struggle to impose their interpretations on everyone as they did in the past? Moises Naim in his book *The End of Power* turns to Max Weber: "Weber argued that, in the past, much authority had been 'traditional'— that is, inherited by its holders and accepted by the holders' subjects."[21]

A second source for authority had been 'charismatic', in which an individual leader was seen by followers to possess a special gift. But the third form of authority—and the one suited to modern times—is 'bureaucratic' and 'rational' authority, grounded in laws and wielded by an administrative structure capable of enforcing clear and consistent rules. It rests, Weber wrote, on the "belief in the validity of legal statute and functional competence based on rationally created rules". This belief in the legitimacy of the bureaucracy and the universal validity of "rationally created rules" started breaking down decades ago and this process is accelerating rapidly today.

There is a growing realization that institutions and bureaucracies are social constructs. Each institution has its own internal culture and its own interests. As a result, there is no such thing as an independent, objective truth that is unchallengeable – something that applies to much of what is presented to the public – from national statistics to scientific orthodoxy. Politicians are fond of underpinning their arguments with 'facts'. But, in today's world, facts and 'evidence' are regularly challenged. Different groups continually present alternative numbers and counter-analyses to make clear that most of what is presented as 'fact' is actually interpretation conditioned by values, vested interest and political perspective. When it is really important, for example during the EU referendum campaign in the UK, there are no agreed facts at all.

In a *Financial Times* article, Angus Deaton, winner of the 2015 Nobel Prize in economics, argues that: "Statistics are far from politics-free; indeed, politics is encoded in their genes."[22] He goes on to argue that this is ultimately a good thing. The same applies to the world of science, as perfectly illustrated by the debate around climate change, an area of significant scientific uncertainty, where the battle for people's hearts and minds has clearly shifted from a discussion about the science, and the uncertainty surrounding it, to a power battle between alternative interpretations and conflicting political imperatives. It is the evolution of power structures, not science, that will ultimately determine how we respond to the largely unanswerable questions raised by climate science.

Another issue undermining the trust in institutions is that our current institutions – from universities to the civil service, from political parties to charities, from central banks to the European Union – have all been built in the modern mode. They are top-down, centralized power structures that are finding it difficult to adapt rapidly to the twenty-first century world. As Niall Ferguson elaborates in *The Great Degeneration*, they are no longer fit for purpose – something that has not escaped the intuitive instinct of the public.

It is easy to react to this undermining of authority with despondency, seeing it as the end of the world order as we have known it. But any Liberal could welcome these cultural developments. Breaking down the tyranny of imposed authority has always been at the core of Liberal politics. Contemporary culture once again captures that spirit, and forward-looking Liberal parties should welcome it and seize the opportunities it offers for a Liberal revival.

We now find ourselves once more in a situation like the one after the French Revolution. We can see that it is easy to criticize, undermine and even destroy existing institutions that are not fit for purpose. Yet, as the Arab Spring has clearly shown, it is easier to tear down than to imagine and build something new. And this remains the case whether the tearing down was done by the populace or by 'those who know what's best', as we have seen in Iraq and Afghanistan. The political challenge is to re-imagine our institutions and fundamentally re-cast them in a new mould fit for the twenty-first century, even as they fight tooth and nail against change. Liberals are the only ones who can achieve changes like that, because most others are, to a greater or lesser extent, captured by those very institutions that need to be transformed.

## Geography

As we outlined earlier, the nation state has been the dominant entity of the modern age. Politics and government are consequently structured around nations and gain their legitimacy from them. At a more granular level, society was also structured geographically. Streets, villages, towns, cities and regions formed cohesive social units determined by geography.

This is one reason why the British army used to be structured around regiments that drew from the same geographical base. It made sure of a level of cohesion that could not be achieved in any other way. This geographical focus brought both advantages and issues over the centuries. Locally, neighbourhoods created a sense of social cohesion, fraternity, solidarity and mixing of the social classes.

The difficulty was that the nation state, and its continually shifting borders, attempted to bury other drivers of social cohesion such as those based on tribe, ethnicity or history. Nations embarked on wars for territory or resources. Locally, fissures developed as social groups – whether they were defined by ethnicity, wealth or other commonalities – tended to congregate, creating wealthy suburbs, slums for the poor, no-go crime ridden zones and ethnic groups concentrated in their own areas. All evidence of the fact that the desires and behaviours of ordinary people were totally at odds with the elite's version of what a globalized world should look like.

While the importance of geography has not, and will not,

disappear, it is under obvious strain. As business and financial flows became first trans-national and then global, the political structure, which remained national, became increasingly misaligned with the functioning of economies, which have become increasingly trans-national. This increasing disconnect between political legitimacy and economic structure is one of the biggest issues our societies face today. Culturally it creates feelings of uncertainty, delegitimization and even fear among many – especially those who feel that globalization is leaving them behind, dependent on a nationally based set of institutions that cannot, or will not, look after their interests.

Below the level of the nation state, the role of geography has also changed. Today, many choose which communities they belong to online – communities of cyber-friendship, shared beliefs and shared interests – while neighbourhood becomes a less important driver of community. While geography remains important when people interact with or within local institutions – hospitals, schools, sports clubs and the like – an increasing sense of community is being formed, which is sometimes more independent of geography. Ease of travel further undermines the importance of locality. Many now work at distance – either traveling to work or online – creating a disconnect between their work and home environments. There is little doubt that, today, geography continues to play a very significant role in local affairs. How much it will remain so is yet to be seen. But while it remains relatively strong, there are opportunities for it to be harnessed as the power of geography wanes at the national level.

## A New World Order

Recognizing the move towards a more interconnected world, the post-war global elite envisioned a new world order. Countries would co-operate to devise a system of 'global governance' where a set of clear rules would be agreed upon, everyone would abide by them and stability and certainty would reign. International institutions – the League of Nations (later the UN), the IMF, the World Bank, NATO, Bretton Woods, the European Economic Community (later the EU) – were the poster children of the new world order. In this new world, globalization would be a positive. It would interlink economies, diminish the chances of conflict and spread prosperity around the globe. The international elite would be in charge and would steer the whole globe to peace and prosperity.

The trouble is that these institutions were set up in a perfectly modern mould even as modernity was starting to fray at the edges. They are top down bureaucracies run by people supposedly endowed with superior skills that, they felt, verged on infallibility. They favoured technocracy over democratic legitimacy and accountability. Most of them did little to hide their obvious disdain for the wider populace – the great unwashed. The narrative was that if the wider populace could only be 'educated' then they would think just like the elite.

There is, of course, nothing inherently wrong in turning to those who are expert in their field when making decisions in a complex world. Issues do, however, arise. These are well summarized by Robert Frank in *Listen Liberal: Or What Ever Happened to the Party of the People*: "Rule-by-expert, it began to seem, excluded rule-by-the-people. It was dehumanizing and mechanical. In a technocracy, the important policy decisions were made in faraway offices that were insulated from the larger whirl of society. The people making the decisions identified far more with society's rulers than they did with the ruled, and their decisions often completely ignored public concerns."[23] In other words, issues arise when the experts stop seeing themselves as social trustees and start seeing themselves either as the rulers' lackeys or as rulers themselves answerable only to their peers.

While the work of these technocratic institutions has brought undoubted and significant benefits, they have never had, and still today do not have, any means of connecting with the voting public for whom they are at best seen as irrelevant, at worst as yet another tool through which the global elite can advance their own interests at their expense. Rather than evolving into the fast, flexible, people-empowering networks that are now required for tomorrow's world, these institutions remain stuck in the same mindset as when they were founded. They combine the inflexible, technocratic, top-down approach of a modern bureaucracy with less political legitimacy than the nation state they were intended to supersede.

These institutions also epitomize the arrogant hubris of the modern. The idea that an increasingly complex, unpredictable world of human beings driven by a complex web of values and emotions can be technocratically managed by a few bright people in fancy offices dotted around the globe. As these institutions increasingly, and predictably, struggle with the complex challenges of today's world – challenges that cannot easily be codified into some kind of clear political taxonomy – their missteps continue to mount. One example has been the total mishandling of the Greek debt crisis by the technocratic troika of the IMF, the ECB and the European Commission, where technocratic mismanagement has destroyed the lives of millions of people and brought a whole country to its knees – something now clearly recognized by the

IMFs own internal auditors.

These changes in the relevance of geography are important for Liberals who have traditionally seen themselves as the champions of both localism and internationalism, and for good reasons – they provide and protect that vital challenge from below that Popper set out. Yet the meaning of the words 'localism' and 'internationalism', in so far as they have practical meaning, has changed dramatically as has the effectiveness or otherwise of traditional policy approaches to them. Traditional modern approaches clearly no longer work. A resurgent Liberalism will need to invent new approaches that match these social and cultural changes. Both localism and internationalism need to be re-defined.

## Identity

We have all seen them – and largely hated them. The modernist buildings in the international style represent highly efficient use of space and materials but are devoid of soul. They mostly look the same (bad) with no individual identity. As in buildings, so in society. Loss of identity has been one of the most destructive effects of the modern.

In modernist thinking, people became cogs in the great societal machine. Previously important determinants of identity – religion, tribe, ethnicity, culture, locality, social class, even, to some extent, family and nation – have all been undermined, declared irrational and sacrificed at the altar of progress.

But people need a strong sense of identity. They need to feel they belong. So, of course, we are seeing the rapid emergence of new political parties that offer identity politics. Many of the elite dismiss these new parties as populist, xenophobic hatemongers. That is to misunderstand that they are filling an important cultural and emotional vacuum left by the excesses of the efficient, rational modern. Combining identity politics with their ability to capitalize on the outdated nature of our institutions and the undermining of authority described above, these insurgents have, over the last twenty years or so, morphed from fringe parties to major political forces that are transforming politics and society. Their rise was enabled by the vacuum left by mainstream parties which either considered the politics of identity as undesirable and retrograde or, if they recognized its importance, were unable to come up with an effective response of their own.

In 1994, Sir Vince Cable wrote a pamphlet arguing that the slow decline of the politics of Right versus Left was leading to the emergence of a new politics of identity. In an updated version in 2005, he argued: "identity will help to reshape the landscape of parties and political ideas in Britain and... we face a shared challenge in finding ways to live with identity politics which preserve open and inclusive approaches to politics and society."

Here we are unable to explore the politics of identity in the same level of detail or with the same level of skill as in Cable's pamphlets, which interested readers can explore for themselves.[24] But it is enough to suggest that identity is essential to what makes us human. The modern tried to airbrush identity out of existence or transform it into something rational and utilitarian rather than what it really is – something that is cultural, visceral and deeply emotional. All this was done with good intentions. In a globalized world, national and sub-national identities were considered a hindrance to progress and, more locally, identity was equated with class wars, religious intolerance, ghettoization and all manner of other evils. Progress was to turn us all into rational global citizens, looking beyond the parochial to the global. In other words, the richness of culture, history and specific identities were all to be subordinated to the common global culture. We were all to change from citizens with complex, deeply rooted identities to plain vanilla.

What we failed to see was that such a journey only resonated with a miniscule proportion of the population – the Liberal cosmopolitan elite for whom even the obvious differences between men and women were to be denied. For the vast majority it felt like being robbed of who they were in an attempt to create a homogenized mush. Sooner or later, some kind of rejection was inevitable.

Putting people in environments where they are expected to subordinate deeply felt identities to a common, imposed identity actually leads people to assert their individuality by emphasizing their differences. Put an engineer and an artist in the same room and their behaviour – from their clothing to whether they turn up on time to how they choose to conduct the meeting – immediately turn into an assertion of their own individual identity. Nick Clegg relates how, when he became a Member of the European Parliament, he expected to enter an environment that was 'European'. What he found instead was that MEPs tended to behave in ways that emphasized their own national identities and highlighted national stereotypes, almost to the point of caricature.

The politics of identity represent a normal human response to the unemotional plain vanilla attitude of the modern. Fighting against what some consider the less desirable elements of this politics will fail if it just denies this, or tries to airbrush identity out of existence. Instead, it means we have to understand the changing meaning of identity in our contemporary culture and develop a politics that turns its energy into a positive social force.

For Liberals, addressing the issues related to identity will likely prove a most difficult challenge. Other political parties have a base of support that is, in part, based on identity. Many businesspeople in the UK support the Conservative Party without giving it much thought. It seems to be almost automatic – a matter of identity as a successful business person – that one identifies as a Conservative. Similarly, there will always be a substantial base of people who consider themselves to be 'working class' for whom support for the Labour Party is part of their identity. The same is true in most other countries. Liberals often lack any strong political base built on identity.

The traditional open-minded, cross-cultural, international outlook of Liberalism tends to make Liberals allergic to identity politics, though there are exceptions – some kinds of liberation and nationalisms have always appealed to Liberals. Yet without recognizing the fundamental human importance of identity, its resurgence in contemporary culture and developing a clear identity politics that has broad appeal, Liberalism can neither mount a resurgence, nor can it be politically effective against the divisive elements of today's identity politics.

## Participation

From cultural products to consumer products, from politics to healthcare, something else is happening that is fundamentally changing expectations of how things should work. The idea of individuals as 'consumers', provided with a market-driven choice of pre-prepared and pre-packaged products, is rapidly breaking down. Today's expectation is that individuals are no longer 'consumers', but they want to be co-producers of the products and services they consume. The modern idea of mass-production, where the consumer's say was limited to one of making a choice among an array of standardized products, is starting to fade. Instead, we are seeing the rise of participation in production as an integral part of the product and service being offered, what Alvin Toffler first described as 'pro-sumers'.

At its simplest level, many of us no longer expect to go out and buy a standard computer off the shelf. Rather we expect to go online and construct the best combination of parts that suits our needs. In the future, we may not ever buy a physical product but we may interact and modify broadly conceived designs that we tailor to our own taste and needs and, having co-designed the product, we will fire up our home 3D printer to produce it.

Such co-production is now everywhere. TV shows like Big Brother cannot exist without the participation of the audience. Newspapers and news programmes now routinely 'crowdsource' content with Twitter feeds, reader comments and all other manner of popular participation. Asking people who happen to be on site to contribute their videos or photographs is supplementing and, who knows may eventually replace, the traveling news photographer or videographer. An increasing proportion of people have moved beyond going to their doctor to be told how their condition is best treated. With the help of medical websites, apps and a newly found popular confidence, people define their own treatment plans for which their doctor is but one input. This is changing the dominance of the modern idea of 'evidence-based' treatment protocols defined by the experts and through which patients are supposed to flow seamlessly like mince in a sausage factory.

In education, the top-down imposition of a rigid curriculum seems as outdated as the horse-drawn hansom cab. Individuals can now design their own education and draw different modules from the best that is available online from anywhere across the globe. In music, the artist-dominated album has long given way to the individually constructed playlists and, going further, users now mix and match stems from different pieces of music to create their own songs and tracks. Members and donors of political parties are no longer content to pay their way and wait for those at the top of the party to define strategy and policy. They expect to take part in the process.

Institutions will, and do, of course resist developments like this. It took a friend who is a professor of occupational medicine five years to persuade his institution to allow him to offer a modular postgraduate course – and when permission was granted, it was grudging and with some considerable anxiety. Once again, it was seen as threatening to the self-identity of the broader faculty that sees itself as knowing what's best for everyone – a threat that was hidden behind the usual tiresome protestations of a threatened collapse in the quality of education. Similarly, in the UK, Conservative ministers continue to push standardized national curricula in the belief that only they know what's best for every single child in the land.

Of course, such a newly found confidence brings threats as well as opportunities. In the Middle East, ISIS has decided it can build its own caliphate irrespective of any form of internationally agreed borders or the views of the international community and international institutions. Political groups driven by their own ideology no longer feel they have to submit to the direction decided by any party leadership. They can simply set up their own grouping within a party to exercise influence – such as the Tea Party inside the Republican Party – or else produce a separate party of their own.

In politics, this cultural change has major implications that range from how political parties are run to the role of government in society, to the way that public services are structured and provided. Once again, this change is inherently Liberal and should provide those Liberals who can harness it with immense opportunities. But it requires a re-definition of what it means for parties that may be smaller than their dominant counterparts to grow up. They need to understand that growing up in a contemporary world means doing things differently, rather than copying the culture, attitude and ways of doing things of the political parties that are still dominant.

Alan Kirby, in an article titled *The Death of Postmodernism and Beyond*, calls this new culture post-post-modernism or pseudo-modernism.[25] He argues that: "The terms by which authority, knowledge, selfhood, reality and time are conceived have been altered, suddenly and forever."

He goes on to describe the culture of participation in the context of cultural products as follows: "Postmodernism conceived of contemporary culture as a spectacle before which the individual sat powerless, and within which questions of the real were problematized... Its successor, which I will call pseudo-modernism, makes the individual's action the necessary condition of the cultural product." Replace 'cultural product' with physical product, healthcare, politics, government, public services, education, financial services or whatever else and the same analysis applies.

Whether we agree with this definition of what comes after postmodernism or not, the world is changing, and the big question at the heart of the new age of an atomized society and atomized production is: what is that will hold us together again? If modernism was a reaction against the lies and half-truths of the

First World War, and a project to find truth, post-modernism was a reaction against neatness, industrial systems and assembly line thinking. The new emerging age will be a reaction against the hollowness of the post-modern world, the reductionism of our one-dimensional systems and shiny, one-dimensional culture. It will be a reaction against the virtual mesh without individual authors or creativity, where real and unreal blur together – where individuals are hopelessly isolated in mutual misunderstanding and cultural barriers.

As the American philosopher Robert Nozick put it "In a virtual world, people will long for reality even more."[26]  That search for reality, and the depth that lies behind it, is the grand project of the age that is to come. That is a project that is tailor-made for Liberals.

## Spirituality

What is a section on spirituality doing in a book on Liberalism? After all has secularization and breaking down the manacles of religion and its hold on power not been a defining feature of Liberal philosophy for centuries?

Yes, of course it has, though in the UK it has tended to go hand in hand with the non-conformist tradition. But after the modern age, spirituality is making a comeback; spirituality, that is, which is different from religion. Embracing the new spirituality is a project of the age that is to come. It is a project that demands depth, and it offers Liberals significant opportunities.

We shall start by defining what we mean by spirituality in the context of contemporary culture. Religion is, of course, one form of spirituality. Religion is a community endeavour. It is based on a codified system of beliefs and rules and, in organized religions, often a power hierarchy. But in the contemporary world, we mean something quite different by spirituality. In the late 1990s, the psychologist Daniel Helminiak expanded the traditional definitions of spirituality to include what human beings strive for to give meaning, purpose and connection to their life. For some, this may also extend to a need for transcendence – the sense that something in life goes beyond the here and now.[27]

Helminiak thus takes spirituality beyond religion to a broader concept that, he argues, is inherent to human nature. Following the enforced rationality of the modern, and the determined irrationality of postmodernism, we are seeing a revival of such a human need for purpose and meaning – what we believe is a kind of spirituality.

In some cases, this revival is expressed in the context of the beliefs and structures of organized religion. Some of these have positive consequences while others have turned extreme, descending into the violence and terrorism that we are all witnessing today. In these cases, as we have outlined above, religion is more an expression of identity than it is an expression of spirituality. But we are also seeing a more widespread manifestation of Helminiak's interpretation of spirituality – the need for a meaning and purpose beyond the here and now, a concern with non-materialistic values and a search for a broader and deeper perspective on life, the need for some kind of moral compass that goes beyond the hollowness of a worldly utilitarianism.

This is manifesting itself in many, varied ways – from the widespread spiritual or semi-spiritual practices such as yoga, meditation, and the spread of *ayahuasca* spiritual experiences, to the increasing use of mindfulness as a personal development technique in companies such as Google, to a number of corporations exploring their larger social purpose beyond providing shareholder returns, to the significant rise in the amounts of money flowing into investments that provide broader social returns in addition to financial returns. These and many other developments that we see all around us are, like the search for identity described above, symptoms of a cultural move beyond the bland utilitarianism of the modern to a search for something more meaningful. While many do not choose organized religion as a route to meaning, it is nevertheless noticeable how religious leaders such as Pope Francis have today achieved a public and political resonance well beyond their own faithful – something that was unimaginable at the height of the rational modern.

What might this mean for Liberalism? Certainly the rise of repressive religious fundamentalism that we are witnessing does not bode well for Liberal attitudes. Neither does the seemingly increasing strength of the religious Right in the United States. But neither of these developments is yet pronounced in Europe where the new spirituality is largely secular and highly personal.

The danger is that Liberals might automatically associate any form of spirituality with an illiberal attitude. Nothing could be further from the truth. Experiments done in the Department of Psychology at the University of Toronto found that, while religious individuals tend to be more conservative, spiritual people tend to be more Liberal (in the North American sense of the word). They also found that inducing a spiritual experience through guided meditation led both Liberals and conservatives to endorse more Liberal political attitudes.

Liberalism has the opportunity to benefit from these changing attitudes if it can re-discover the time when Liberal politics was itself driven by a strong sense of higher purpose beyond the banal retail politics of today, and can manage to look beyond organized religion to the broader understanding of spirituality that we describe here.

## The firm

The modern large firm is one of the most powerful political institutions in today's world. Throughout the age of the modern, large companies have transformed themselves from profit-seeking entities into political entities. Even as many business leaders publically declare themselves to be apolitical, they and their firms today wield more political power than they ever have.

From manipulating governments through threats of disinvestment unless they implement 'business-friendly' policies, to their impact on people's lives through their terms of employment, they are active in the policy world. Like the amount of tax that they choose to pay in any particular jurisdiction. Or the impact of political donations on party policy. Or the amount of public money consumed by subsidies. Or the increasing dependence of charitable and other public institutions such as scientific research bodies, museums and the like on corporate donations. Or their direct influence on the structure of cross-national policies such as trade agreements. Or the pressure they (under the guise of 'the markets') are able to exert directly on debt-burdened governments. In these ways, and others, the political influence of today's multinational corporations is considerable.

A fictitious *Harvard Business Review* case study about a company struggling with whether it was wise to make political donations, when candidates they support might change their policy positions overnight, contains this quote from the CEO: "Do you think I would've gotten a meeting with the governor on 24-hour notice if we hadn't been a donor?"[28] When board members critical of the company's direct involvement in politics argued that other companies do not get involved in politics but were still successful his response was "but those companies *are* in politics. They're just involved in ways that don't leave those obvious 'receipts' lying around for the national media to find."

It is worth noting that such political influences are not limited to multinational firms. Smaller companies that may be of national importance, ultra high net worth individuals, large international NGOs and organized trade unions all, in effect, exert similar influences as much as they can.

In the modern world, it is hardly right to think of firms as apolitical entities. They are intensely political. They form part of our political structure and should be considered as part of the panoply of political institutions. Protestations that they are simply part of 'the market', operating at arms-length from government, are fake and should be treated as such. Businesses may try hard to be non-partisan – knowing full well that they have to be able to exert influence on governments of any colour. But that does not make them in any way apolitical.

None of this needs to be met with moral indignation or outrage, simply with the recognition that politics, commerce and other forms of organized vested interests are all inextricably intertwined and that assertions to the contrary should be ignored.

The cultural position of large firms is, however, also changing rapidly. The social contract between corporations and their employees has all but disappeared. The relationship between the large firm, its employees and the communities in which it operates, is now usually a short-term, pragmatic, contractual one.

Employees are fired largely at will when the financial situation of the firm demands it. Firms are willing to abandon communities as soon as it is convenient to move operations elsewhere. As a result, bonds of loyalty between firms, communities and individuals have all but disappeared. The scams and scandals that we witness daily are the work of a minority of players. But they receive widespread media attention and have further undermined confidence in the firm as an agent of good.

At a cultural level, the brand value of the large firm has also decreased. A generation ago, young graduates were proud to get a job with IBM, Barclays or a large accountancy firm. Today the cool thing to achieve is to work for an insurgent startup or, even better, to start your own business. That is where the best young talent is now to be found.

Even as a minority of business leaders continue to show their lack of leadership by presiding over scandals and rotten corporate cultures, the younger generation and some far-sighted business leaders are starting social enterprises and B-Corporations or building social responsibility into the framework of their business, as opposed to those who are merely setting up CSR programmes in order to be able to tick the box while proceeding with business as usual.

These cultural developments carry significant opportunities for Liberals. In a recent pamphlet we published, *A Radical Politics for Business*, we argued that: "What has happened is that the major energy of business has shifted behind radical change."[29] Liberals have always been the agents of change, which is why we also argued in our pamphlet that "business is returning to its original Liberal roots". These changes, combined with the traditional Liberal support for the insurgent against the incumbent, means that the cultural changes affecting the firm provide a good substrate for a Liberal revival – if Liberals are able to capture and capitalize on the *zeitgeist*.

But to do this, Liberals must also abandon the idea that firms operate in the mythical free market and are separate from politics and government. They are not and they should be treated as much as political institutions as they are seen as private agents.

## What does all this mean for Liberalism?

There are a number of strands in this chapter, but the message is similar for each of them: *the world is changing*. The modernist assumptions our generation was brought up with are crumbling. Some of the implications of this, like the fragmentation of the nation state and the decline of state and international institutions, are fraught with difficulty. There are certainly trends that ought to worry Liberals, it is true. But, in our view, the composite picture that emerges from our cultural meander is that more of the cultural trends that we see emerging tend to support a Liberal revival rather than the death of Liberalism.

The big question is whether Liberals will be able to capitalize on these changes or whether they will be marginalized by other political forces that are better able to capture the energy of contemporary culture and direct it to their own ends. To be successful, Liberals will need to forge a better understanding of a changing world and be willing to transform themselves and their Liberal politics into something that is in tune with the changing cultural landscape. To do this, politicians of all stripes who consider themselves Liberal will need to re-discover the ability to feel in their guts the changing cultural landscape and what it means for the values and feelings of the citizen.

Liberalism has traditionally had the understanding of the depth of human beings, and of authentic human needs. It now needs to re-discover that understanding to succeed in a twenty-first century culture. But much of that gut feel for contemporary culture has been destroyed in what we might call the amateur professionalization of politics – the modern idea that market research, analysis and polling charts should totally replace political instinct. As Drew Westen aptly puts it in *The Political Brain*: "In the twenty-first century, the exclusive reliance on polling and focus groups is no longer tenable. These methods can't dig deep enough to assess [the workings of brain] networks that people either don't know about or don't want to admit, whether to a pollster, a group of strangers in a focus group, or themselves."[30]

The ability to feel the currents and counter-currents making contemporary culture and risking a de-stabilization, and maybe collapse, of our politics and our institutions will require much more than retail politics driven by polls and focus groups.

If Liberals are to succeed in preserving our liberal societies rather than surrendering them, it is in their commitment to the primacy of individual human beings operating within communities (however defined), and their ability to challenge from below, that will provide a clear way forward for Liberals. But there are certainly aspects of traditional Liberal thought that are now outdated and no longer have either relevance or resonance. These will need to be re-interpreted or jettisoned. Working out what all this means and how to meet these challenges and succeed is what the rest of this book is about.

# 4

# The changing dimensions of the globe

*"Ideas, knowledge, art, hospitality, travel - these are the things which should of their nature be international. But let goods be homespun whenever it is reasonably and conveniently possible; and, above all, let finance be primarily national."*
**John Maynard Keynes, 1933**

Unthinking cheerleaders for an undefined internationalism. This is how may Liberals come across to us – and doubtless to many other voters.

The speech by the great Liberal economist John Maynard Keynes to the Irish government in 1933, known as 'National Self-sufficiency', is largely ignored and forgotten among economists. It doesn't reflect the prevailing orthodoxy that now suppresses so much innovation in policy-making circles.

But the speech is also one of those very rare things, a piece of literature – soaring writing – by an economist, and one who was not quite yet at the height of his fame. In the speech, he talked about some of the key questions that face us even more powerfully today, around how much nations should be open to the outside world and how closed and protective they ought to be of their own economies and cultures.

Keynes saw clearly that these are different questions and that single answers don't work very well. He said instead that:

"I sympathize, therefore, with those who would minimize, rather than with those who would maximize, economic entanglement between nations. Ideas, knowledge, art, hospitality, travel - these are the things which should of their nature be international. But let goods be homespun whenever it is reasonably and conveniently possible; and, above all, let finance be primarily national. Yet, at the same time, those who seek to disembarrass a country of its entanglements should be very slow and wary. It should not be a matter of tearing up roots but of slowly training a plant to grow in a different direction. For these strong reasons, therefore, I am inclined to the belief that, after the transition is accomplished, a greater measure of national self-sufficiency and economic isolation between countries than existed in 1914 may tend to serve the cause of peace, rather than otherwise. At any rate the age of economic internationalism was not particularly successful in avoiding war; and if its friends retort that the imperfection of its success never gave it a fair chance, it is reasonable to point out that a greater success is scarcely probable in the coming years."[31]

This is the passage which has attracted such deep disapproval in recent years, as if Keynes had somehow embraced the protectionism which contributed to the outbreak of the Second World War, by deepening the Great Depression. On the contrary, Keynes saw clearly that economic internationalism, as he put it, was not very successful at avoiding war in 1914, and that the ability of nations and communities to develop economies that can provide for some of their own needs – a very different matter to protectionism – might allow them to thrive with a measure of peaceful independence. He was right, of course, that peace was "scarcely probable in the coming years". He was, after all, speaking just as Hitler was coming to power in Germany.

But the distinction Keynes draws between those elements of modern life that enhance civilization by making them international, and those which need to be local as far as possible, is an important one. Ideas, knowledge, art, hospitality, travel should be international, he said, but "let goods be homespun whenever it is reasonably and conveniently possible". The modern globalization ideology purports to be Liberal but is blind to this important distinction. Often it has meant, in practice, not so much free trade as compulsory trade – of the kind, enforced by debt, which the Romans and colonial Spanish and the British in India, imposed on their captive populations.

Keynes' distinction also implies the other ways in which globalization has in practice proved illiberal. Although it gathered to itself the trappings of internationalism, lulling Liberals without a proper grasp of their own ideology into reassuring sleep, globalization has in practice meant the process by which governments handed their own powers to corporations. It was not about reducing the power of the state, as Liberals believed: it was about diverting it.

It was true that government powers were often misused and tyrannical, but they are no less so when wielded by corporate lawyers. Perhaps most dangerously for self-determination and democracy, the new investor states disputes procedures allow companies to sue governments for taking democratic decisions which undermine their investments – most recently, the oil company Occidental extracted $2.8 billion from Ecuador for annulling the contract between them. If these procedures limit themselves to agreements directly with nations, then that is arguable. But if they stray into issues of which chemicals should be allowed, then that is the precise opposite of Liberalism. The risks of abuse are so certain, and so extreme, that the future of TTIP and other trade agreements are threatened as a result.

The problem is that the world according to 'neoliberal' globalization is blind to imbalances in economic power – the main purpose behind free trade in its original, rather than its current form. As it stands now, neoliberal free trade threatens to plunge us into an illiberal, Hobbesian world, where only the richest and most powerful can survive.

## Europe

This ignorance of their own intellectual heritage is a threat to European Liberalism, just as it is in the UK. The idea of a collaborative Europe working together for the greater good of the continent is, perhaps, one of the greatest, most powerful and most ambitious political projects ever undertaken. What angers those of us who believed the dream is how it has been reduced in its implementation. It is especially so in its failure to rise to the challenge of a new kind of economics, and the gap allowed Liberals to embrace a scheme that has let the spectre of fascism seep back into western Europe.

This is brought into sharp focus in the Liberal support for the disastrous single currency scheme for Europe – the poster child of an ever more centralized Europe that goes against everything that Liberals should stand for.

*The disaster of single currencie*

Keynes called gold a 'barbarous relic', but – even after Gordon Brown sold off the UK gold reserves at rock bottom prices – the single currency in Europe was a symptom of the same kind of gold-standard thinking: it is about the illusion of the stability of value and about strong money. It is an extension of German *Ordnungspolitik* with its belief in "sound money", supply side economics that eschews any form of demand side stimulus, and the simplistic treatment of national finances as though they were nothing more than household budgets. It is an approach that is fundamentally mercantilist, and therefore incompatible with harmony between nations, and that abhors the use of debt (in German, the word for debt, *schuld*, is identical to the word for blame or guilt).

In 1925, the British Chancellor of the Exchequer Winston Churchill described a system of international currencies which "vary together, like ships in harbour whose gangways are joined and who rise and fall together with the tide". This was a description of gold standard money on the eve of the world's return to it. It was a famously disastrous decision, instrumental in the Great Depression and therefore in the Second World War. When you use gold as the basis for money, it tends to favour the rich and impoverish the poor. It is the same with the euro.

It does so because changing the value of your currency, and varying your interest rate, for example, is the way that disadvantaged places are able to make their goods more affordable. When you stop them from doing that, you trap whole cities and regions – the poorest people in the poorest places – without being able to trade their way out. Of course, the USA has one currency and so does Britain. But that has hardly been satisfactory either.

But, in the USA and the UK, unlike in Europe, the issues of a single currency can be mitigated to some extent through major transfers in resources between regions – though such resource shifts have rarely proved sufficient. These shifts become necessary because central banks set their interest rates to favour their big cities. In the UK, we have interest rates set to suit the City of London, while the manufacturing regions of the north struggle as best they can. Across Europe, the effects have been so much worse. That was always the danger of the euro: it meant success for the areas that are already successful. It meant a real struggle for the great reviving cities like Liverpool and Warsaw or countries like Greece and Portugal. The single currency also traps countries into issuing debt in a currency over which they have no control – with the disastrous consequences that we have seen.

All this is because single currencies are not the universal measuring rods they claim to be. One of the authors of this book said this at a conference on the euro in London in 2000, and the audience reacted with a kind of horror – a Belgian economist in the audience got up in his seat and theatrically spread out his arms in an expression of disbelief. But the truth is that much of what we most value about our own communities and cultures normally fail to show up in money measurement, and – the bigger the currency – the less it shows up. There is no way that the kind of pro-human, pro-inspiration, pro-local ethic of Liberalism can mesh with this kind of gold standard, single yardstick way of thinking.

Part of the problem is that, in a modern economy – even in a modern city – there is really more than one economy at work, and large currencies will never suit them all very accurately. Everyone in London – nurses and currency traders – have to get by using the one currency, the value of which is decided by tens of thousands of youthful traders in braces in Wall Street and the City. That is fine for the international economy and the financial services sector. But there are other economies in cities which feed off the pickings from the rich table above it, but aren't necessarily part of it. These are the economies used by the rest of us, and they cover those aspects of life which have nothing to do with the financial markets.

The international economy brings in executives from all over the world, whose employers will pay their expenses no matter what, forcing up the value of London homes beyond anywhere else in the country, and pricing London services beyond the other economy. So London struggles to employ nurses or teachers or bus drivers because they can't afford to live there, so the basic services suffer. But to keep the economy of Liverpool or East St Louis alive using the same currency alone, you either have to risk inflation in London and New York or you have to make massive money transfers from one region to another – something that is politically all but impossible.

Worse, London's rich economy threatens to drive out the poor economy completely. You can see the same thing happen in offshore financial centres where financial services have priced everything else into oblivion. In places like Jersey in the Channel Isles, offshore finance has worked like a cuckoo in the nest. Jersey's offshore status has made it rich, and yet this was achieved at the expense of Jersey's agriculture and tourist sectors. Why? Because financial services was seen as easy money – a get rich quick scheme that could make Jersey so wealthy that it could afford not to tax its citizens.

The result was an economy structured around one industry – an unsustainable one as it turns out – that drove out everything else and a cost of living that means that nobody but bankers can afford to live and work there. Now that global transparency regulations are threatening the future viability of Jersey's financial sector, there is no other viable economy the jurisdiction can fall back on. There is a third economy in London too, which is also threatened because we are unable to see it. The third economy isn't really an economy at all: it makes up the crucial human transactions that build families and neighbourhoods, look after old people, without which nothing we can do can be successful. Economists call this 'social capital'. The economist Neva Goodwin called it the 'core economy' and market forces don't apply here. Yet without it, the police can't catch criminals, doctors can't heal, children can't be educated and the other economies can't work. This social economy doesn't appear in the GDP, so policy makers assume that it is inexhaustible, so they ignore it.

The problem is that single currencies – whether they are the pound, the dollar or the euro – don't measure the needs and assets in these other economies very accurately. What they miss out gets ignored. Then it gets forgotten. Because currencies are not just measuring systems then, they are eyeglasses. They are the way we see the world. If our currencies value things down, we are unable to see them. If you only measure GDP, then the environment, human dignity, community, family all in the end get slowly driven out. That is what faulty measuring rods do, and currencies are measuring rods. Monocultural money systems drive out other cultures, other species, other languages, other opinions, and other forms of wealth.

As cheerleaders of this flawed idea of a single currency, Liberals, have ended up allowing fascism to enter Europe again. The inevitable euro crisis has pitted one nation against another in a war fought with money rather than bombs and tanks. The economic dangers associated with the introduction of the euro were predictable – and indeed predicted by many, including by us. Yet political leaders at the time chose to make a grand and hubristic political statement irrespective of the devastation it could bring to their citizens. The euro is, maybe, the best example of the consequences of a political and policy elite living in their own world and totally divorced from the consequences of their actions on ordinary people, which is the fundamental problem that history has developed Liberalism to tackle.

The single currency now threatens the continued existence of an international union like the EU, the noble project which helped keep the peace in the most ferocious continent for two generations. The UK needed to be there, though we in this country should also take responsibility for those two other recent changes to the EU which has made it most unpopular: the single market, with its pettifogging regulations, and the expansion to the East. Both were done for excellent reasons, but the way they were done – like the euro – has damaged prospects for the civilized continuation of a brave idea.

Both the single market and the combination of East and West in the same institution are important objectives, but the institutional and democratic framework is still lacking. Liberals began by blaming the vote to leave the EU on ignorance, but it might also be possible to blame it on the failure of the EU to show the kind of flexibility they needed when David Cameron asked for their help, not to mention Jean-Claude Juncker's brainless "no more reform" on the eve of the poll.

*Liberals and the European Union*
The challenge for Liberals now, and not just in the UK, is to

recognize the Liberal roots of the revolt against the EU – it is no coincidence that former Liberal heartlands voted overwhelmingly to leave (Cornwall, Devon, Burnley) – and not to let the only people who are speaking for them be Farage and Le Pen. That also means tackling some particularly critical issues for Liberals across Europe after the results of the British referendum.

Bringing people closer together across the geographical and cultural space known as Europe is a fine Liberal ideal. Its technocratic and undemocratic form of implementation is anything but. And the only people seemingly unable to see this are the Liberal elite.

In his book *Coalition*, former minister David Laws explains how, in the 2014 elections for the European Parliament, Liberal Democrat party strategists had decided to campaign on a strongly pro-EU stance. The results were disastrous with the party losing all but one of its seats. A text message from Norman Lamb, a Liberal Democrat MP, to David Laws read: "Our complacent, uncritical, pro-EU position has once again turned so many of our supporters away."

Laws summarizes the experience as follows: "We had certainly tested to destruction the notion put forward in the past by many of our own MEPs that, if only we campaigned more on our pro-EU position, we would secure a much higher vote share."[32]

Why had these voters abandoned the party? Not, as some would have it, because they were xenophobic racists. But rather because they were Liberals. And any Liberal, while supporting the grand concept of a more united Europe that can work together to address some of the issues that know no national borders, cannot help but be disappointed and even angry at how that lofty ideal has been perverted and corrupted to construct a most illiberal Union. The deafness of today's Liberal elite to the pro-Europe, anti-EU movement that is sweeping Europe is eerily reminiscent of the Liberal collapse in opposition to the suffragettes, the workers' movement and the Irish Independence movement – all Liberal movements resisted by a captured Liberal Establishment. It does nothing but open wide the door to extreme parties that foment division and xenophobia.

*What next for the European Union?*
What next for the EU? There are two elements that make up a potential way forward: institutional reform and re-capturing the original spirit of a united Europe.

First, we need some kind of genuine subsidiarity in the system of government that manages the inherent conflict between internationalism, localism and self-determination better. Membership of the EU made it possible among ethnic groups subsumed within the European nations to set aside the fierce demands of nationalism, but people need a genuine, direct way to manage the affairs of Europe and to feel that they have a say in the way Europe is governed. It is not sustainable as a club for a technocratic elite.

We will not here review all the elements that could form part of the necessary institutional reforms. Interested readers can find an elegant exposition of this in Philippe Legrain's *European Spring: Why our Economies and Politics are in a Mess and How to Put Them Right.*[33] It is time, for example, that people were allowed a direct vote on the composition of the European Commission, including its president, and the president of the European Council, rather than all this being stitched up in the backrooms of Brussels and national capitals in a jobs for the boys (and it does tend to be mainly boys) kind of way.

Yet Liberal democracy is not just about giving the people the right to vote every five years. It is about creating a sense of engagement, a belief that the views of the people matter and that institutions are responsive to the public mood and work for the people's benefit. The EU in its current form fails all these tests. People see EU institutions as remote, incomprehensible and unaccountable. And they see that because that is what they are. We have argued earlier that a Liberal system welcomes challenge from below and responds to such challenge. For the EU nothing could be further from that ideal. Legrain himself has to spend the first part of his book explaining that he is critical of the EU in its current form not because he is anti-European but rather because he is committed to the idea of a Europe that works. This notion that any kind of criticism of the EU is "anti-European" and must be shut down has become widespread. It is an attitude that is antithetical to Liberalism and more reminiscent of the behaviour of paranoid totalitarian regimes the world over.

The EU needs to re-discover – and it has, first of all, to be interested in re-discovering – ways in which its component nation states can be both co-dependent and independent at the same time. A challenge that now also faces the UK as it struggles to devise a new settlement between its component nations.

But institutional reform will need to follow the establishment of a clear vision for a sustainable EU that creates peace, prosperity and a common purpose rather than division, impoverishment of the weak, as well as the enrichment of the powerful and consequent nationalism and fracture. To do this, we need to return to the original vision of the founder Jean Monnet, who believed that Europe needed to be based not so much on trade, but on culture. He understood that three crucial elements were necessary for European success: that the process needed to be gradual – both because it was inherently difficult, and because national cultures could not be seen to be subsumed into a faceless and soulless bureaucracy. He believed that the slow process of creating solidarity among the nations had to precede the creation of common institutions. He also argued that it had to be a Europe of the people not a Europe of technocrats. That is why the Schumann Declaration that established the European Coal and Steel Community in 1950 clearly stated: "Europe will not be made all at once, or according to a single plan. It will be built through concrete achievements which first create a de facto solidarity."

What creates Europe is its traditions in the arts and philosophy, its dynasties and its cultural diversity within a particularly European aesthetic. And above all its humanism and Liberal values. For centuries, these elements have provided the foundation of the transcendent concept that is Europe. A shared identity and set of values that go beyond geography or the ever shifting borders of the individual state or nation. Europe is a humanistic, cultural concept above all else. And today, the fundamental glue that holds Europe together is the transformation of these cultures and traditions into the shared values of Liberal democracy.

That is why countries like Spain, Portugal, Greece, Germany, Italy and the Eastern European states saw their participation in the European project as both a route towards, and a vindication of, their transition from fascist or communist rule to modern Liberal democracies. And that is why we see so much angst surrounding the relationship between Europe and Erdogan's Turkey. Europe's peoples want to preserve and enhance their own distinctive cultures while creating a common space in which Liberal democratic values can thrive.

Yet, all this inspiring richness seems to have been forgotten. The European project has been perverted by a remote, detached technocracy that seems more concerned with accumulating ever more power for its unaccountable institutions and for their pet projects – a single currency, single market regulations and a relentless march towards a deadening, technocratic, bland uniformity that has forgotten Monnet's pleas for gradualism and solidarity as fundamental underpinnings. As a result, our politicians, and our political debate, seem unable to rise above the petty and small-minded concerns of technocracy.

This was maybe never clearer than in the strategy adopted by the failed Remain campaign in the UK's EU referendum. Non-credible and incomprehensible numbers generated by technocrats formed the backbone of the campaign. Little wonder it failed. Where was the inspiration? That was all concentrated in the Leave campaign and its emotional appeal to feelings of national pride and identity and the revival of the spirit of the blitz – we may be on our own but we can do it.

During the Euro crisis of 2013, *Time* magazine quoted IMF chief Christine Lagarde as saying that what Europe needed was "to focus on the long-term backbone of Europe to make it a strong regional, monetary, banking and fiscal institution." Really? Is that all that is left as a long-term backbone of Europe? It is no wonder that the European peoples are turning away from such a limited, pedestrian, insubstantial, dry view of Europe.

Technocrats have taken over from visionary statesmen like Monnet as leaders of the European project and, in the process, they are destroying Europe's soul. And, as clearly expressed by the leader of the European Parliament Martin Schultz: "The moment people withdraw their support from an idea, the idea is finished."And all of this has opened the door for politicians in every single member state to lay at the door of a remote Brussels technocracy every initiative that is perceived as going against the wishes, desires and interests of their own people. Is it any wonder that Euroscepticism is sweeping across the continent?

*Two future visions*

So what is our future vision for a successful Europe of solidarity, shared values, broadly distributed prosperity and open, accountable institutions? There are broadly two visions for the future of the European Union. The first is a vision of the Union as a model built for the challenges of the twentieth century. A Europe at war with itself and challenged by a globalizing world spawned a model of community that transmogrified into a search for ever greater union. From economic community the model has moved rapidly to the search for political union.

We envision a second type of Europe. A Europe of nation states where the role of EU institutions is to oil the wheels of collaboration between different nations. Rather than a federal Europe, such a model envisions a confederation of individual sovereign states. A common framework would allow variable collaborations between different nations on matters of common interest. Groups of countries would be enabled to form alliances and collaborations as and when they see fit. As these collaborations are shown to work (or not), they will serve as a beacon and others may wish to join when the time is right for them. If any particular type of collaboration doesn't work for some, it can be modified or some can retreat as and when they wish.

The role of Brussels then becomes one of service to nation states. Their skill would be to help craft the menu of potential collaborations and provide the know-how and infrastructure to make such alliances work. It is not, as one EU representative to the Netherlands crassly put it to some visiting Americans: "We are the government of Europe." This statement is incorrect but it does betray Brussels' flawed perspective.

This vision is in sharp contrast to that of a centrally led organization seeking to act as one political and economic entity with the individual member states in a role that is largely subordinate to the needs and wishes of the majority. A Europe where twenty-eight or, eventually, more nation states all move together in lock step irrespective of the wide cultural and economic differences that exist, and will continue to exist, between them.

The first vision is based on the twentieth century, centrally managed, top-down bureaucratic organizational model. Politically it is illiberal. It is a model is too unwieldy, too resistant to change and largely unmanageable. It also goes against contemporary cultural mores. It will fail in the twenty-first century – a time that calls for flexibility, opportunities for experimentation in an uncertain world, and the ability to change and respond quickly to rapidly changing circumstances. It is a model that is captured more by the ghosts of Europe's past than by what it will take both to meet the challenges of the future and to inspire its citizens to continue to support the original noble intentions of the European project.

And what of the famed freedom of movement? We believe that a European project that is a cultural expression of its diversity and what holds it together must be underpinned by the right to travel freely across the continent. After all, travel engenders common understanding and brings people closer together. But such freedom to travel should not extend to the unlimited right to draw benefits from public systems into which citizens have not made a meaningful contribution. To say otherwise means a blindness to the economic forces which risk tearing Europe apart.

There is a difference between the freedom to travel and the kind of rootless world where people *have* to travel to make a living. It does not seem to occur to those who defend unlimited freedom of movement that most, though not all, of the people flows that are occurring across the EU are a sign of the failure not the success of the European project. They highlight the continuing economic disparity across nations that the European project has so far failed to correct and, in some instances, has made much worse, which makes travel to foreign countries, leaving friends and family behind, the only way open to millions of people to earn a decent living.

Clearly, for those at the top end of the scale, the opportunity to work in any European country is a pleasure rather than a hardship. As it is for the retired pensioners who can live much better in Spain than in the UK. But these represent a minority and it is not what is causing the major issues arising from uncontrolled movement. It is time that the Liberal elite stopped seeing the world just through their own rose-tinted spectacles and start seeing the world through the eyes of those at the bottom of the heap. As one British Liberal voter (who voted Leave in the referendum) put it, for those at the bottom of the heap, the world looks quite different:

"See, most people working at the bottom end see a load of cheap migrant labour, usually exploited to a greater or lesser degree, and driving down the wages of local people. Now, I'm sure politicians could come up with all sorts of numbers that try and argue that immigration doesn't drive down wages. But the fact is, it probably does, and even if it doesn't then it allows working conditions to be even shitter. Think of the bottom of agricultural and farm work (I'm from the West Country, my cousin is a labourer). Think of migrants sleeping in sheds and shared houses, working excessively long hours doing backbreaking work in fields. Think of shit warehouse jobs along the line of sports direct, clocking in, clocking out, on a zero hours contract. Sick? Tough. There's a migrant who will take your shift. Waitressing, your son breaks his arm? Tough. [A migrant will replace you]."

We have provided our own vision for the future of Europe. Will it come to pass? Sadly, we are doubtful. And for two reasons. We have described the Europe of top-down, technocratic bureaucracy as inflexible and resistant to change. So it is doubtful that it will be able to implement the shift in philosophy necessary for its own revitalization. Getting twenty-eight countries to agree on defining a new direction is a task few may be willing to take on. Then there is the disastrous single currency. Flawed and destructive though it is, it is now embedded. Moving away from it to something resembling common sense may be well nigh impossible though Nobel Prize winning economist Joseph Stiglitz, long a euro critic, suggests that "rule changes needed to make the currency work are in an economic sense small."[34] But making such changes may be politically impossible – particularly while Germany remains the major European political power.

Finally, there is the reality of political folly as described in Barbara Tuchman's previously quoted *The March of Folly* – a book that should be essential reading for all political and policy leaders. She puts it like this:

> "Wooden-headedness, the source of self-deception, is a factor that plays a remarkably large role in government. It consists in assessing a situation in terms of preconceived fixed notions while ignoring or rejecting any contrary signs. It is acting according to wish while not allowing oneself to be deflected by the facts. It is epitomized in a historian's statement about Philip II of Spain, the surpassing wooden-head of all sovereigns: 'No experience of the failure of his policy could shake his belief in its essential excellence.' "[35]

*After Brexit*
What of Britain and Europe? How the Brexit process will unfold is impossible to say. But whichever way it goes, or if it will happen at all, does not diminish from the fact that, while British values are decidedly an uncontestably European, Britain's attitudes to Europe have been, are and will always remain, different to those found in continental countries. British history has been different from that of other European nations. It was not invaded – at least not in any relatively recent times. It has had an uninterrupted democracy for centuries and has not suffered from the fascist and communist periods that have plagued so many European nations.

While the days of empire are long gone, they cannot be airbrushed out of history. Neither can the fact that such history has made Britain look beyond Europe for its trade and diplomatic relations. Britain's involvement in European affairs has been constant and significant. But is has always been by choice – usually a choice to alter the balance of power – rather than through coercion. It has never had a land border with a hostile power. As a result there is simply not the same degree of emotional commitment to the European project in Britain as there is elsewhere. And the British public is unlikely ever to find it in its heart to support a project that descends into illiberalism. Here are some statements from Leave voters as published in the *Guardian*:[36]

"I voted to leave for empowerment, and to feel like my voice is heard and can influence change."

"The EU sacrificed cohesion for expansion."

"Eventually, under the right circumstances, I would like to see us return to the EU, with more visionary and ideologically driven representatives that are forced to make themselves accountable both to their home population and the wider European population."

"For me it was all about sovereignty, the ability to make our own decisions and not be ruled by the faceless, non-elected bureaucrats in Brussels."

"The EU is failing. The euro is collapsing, and the whole EU is going backwards while the rest of the world overtakes."

"I voted because of the almost insurmountable obstacles to reform in Europe... The way the Mediterranean countries have been treated has also been a disgrace."

"The EU is undeniably failing economically, and its principal solution seems to be increasing what is most likely to be causing the failure."

"I... believe in democracy... Whatever the long term outcome for the country, I believe in freedom and self-determination."

These are statements which every Liberal could be proud of. They give the lie to the idea that it was simply xenophobic racism that drove the Leave vote.

That is not to say that we believe that Britain should opt out of playing a major part in European affairs. Of course it should be part of one of the most ambitious projects ever devised. We simply recognize that the historical and cultural substrates on which support for such involvement has to be built among the population must necessarily be different to that which will be successful in other member states. It is this different history and culture that also leads to confusion and ambivalence around Europe among the British Establishment.

Then there was the plan that ought to have happened but never did. The director of European broadcasts at the wartime BBC, the Liberal Noel Newsome, managed to negotiate agreement from most of the warring states of Europe in 1945 to turn Radio Luxembourg into a multinational radio station dedicated to truthful news and cross-European culture. The plan was also backed with enthusiasm by the American government. One of the last acts by the outgoing wartime coalition was to torpedo the plan – another example of the British establishment's fear and confusion over Europe.[37]

## Geopolitics, Trade and Money

Part of the case for leaving the European Union put forward at the recent referendum was that, as a trading nation, we needed at least equal links with the emerging BRICs nations – China, India, Brazil and Russia. There is something to this argument. Trade has underpinned the UK economy for a millennium or more and it has been our ability to trade with the other side of the world that made England the wealthy nation that it is today. If we have a traditional economic speciality, it is finance for trade – finance for manufacturing failed pretty miserably even during the Industrial Revolution, which happened despite the City of London, not because of it.

There are two difficulties with this. One is that free trade agreements are not universally positive. They involve the sharing of sovereignty, as they do in the European single market. The Vote Leave camp suggested that it would be simple to organize a transatlantic agreement with the USA. Maybe it would, but they forget that the current TTIP draft agreement has as many hostages to the loss of sovereignty as the Maastricht Treaty, in particular the controversial and potentially illiberal Investor-States Disputes mechanism of secret courts (see above).

The other problem with extending trading rights to the BRICs nations is that, actually, UK exports have been in terminal decline now for a generation – the victim of the concentration on financial services, the obsession with property, and the failure (first identified by the government's Macmillan Report in 1930) of the City to understand the needs of exporters and manufacturers. Reaching the BRICs countries will mean tackling the unbalanced economy here before anything else will work.

None of these issues were discussed as part of the European

referendum, as if they were somehow beyond politics. Or as if the real issue – behind all the argument and verbiage – was not about whether or not we should be a member of the European Union, but whether a small group of Conservative Party rebels should be allowed to seize the nation and rule without constraint. As we have outlined, the EU is an imperfect mechanism, but so would be a series of trade agreements managed by the elite.

Nor did the debate address the great issue of our times, which is how we shape a global economy that is able both to maximize wealth but also to provide for the reasonable aspirations of the vast majority of the planet, and without overwhelming the planetary limits either. These issues remain unaddressed by Westminster and they are becoming increasingly important, as it becomes clear that – on present trends – only the very rich are able to reap the benefits of the economy, which is geared in their favour. And as IT does away with working class jobs, skilled jobs, and increasingly professional jobs too, this trend will only get worse.

Some other solution is necessary and it is our contention that it is the Liberal destiny across Europe to set it out and make it happen – to propose mechanisms that can allow people to earn what they need, or provide them with the spending power they need, and on what basis, perhaps by ending the traditional link – which no longer applies to the ultra-rich – between income and employment. What that solution might be we address in the next chapter.

How can we make the next great step forward for economics, so that the economy – rather than government control – provides for the civilized lives of most people? That is the central question and it is impossible to separate that from other geopolitical issues and the changing shape of the world. That does not mean that trade policy somehow subsumes other ethical imperatives, but trade is still – as it traditionally was – the main framework by which Liberals see the world. It is just that Liberals regard local trade and local business as just as important, if not more important, than the mega-deals that politicians so love.

Part of the problem is that what seemed like globalization was actually a massive over-simplification of the world, by appearing to flatten values, and by pricing everything in dollars or a handful of other international currencies. If single currencies are gold standard thinking, applying limited vision to a complex world (see above), then that is a reminder that we need a multiplicity of yardsticks, which recognize the importance of local life and culture. That is likely to mean a multiplicity of cultures and languages. It is also going to mean a multiplicity of currencies within and between the same nations, some exchangeable, some not. That is how cultures can balance each other's economies effectively.

Some of those currencies will be international, like Keynes' *bancor*. Some of them will underpin ecological progress by taking on the value of basic commodities. Some will allow nations within nations to look after their own populations, like the proposed Scotpound.[38] Some will borrow from the old medieval 'black money' which supported the economies of cities or cathedrals, and which lost value rather than gained it, to encourage spending.[39] Some will be social currencies which manage what we owe the communities or the educational establishments we belong to.[40] These can be managed by mobile phones in a way that was impossible even ten years ago.

Most of all, we need new kinds of local financial institutions, designed to support entrepreneurs, and which can provide credit in parallel currencies, like the WIR system in Switzerland, or Sonantes in Nantes, or the network of community banks backed by the Brazilian central bank.[41]

It is also worth remembering that not even these measurement systems will accurately reflect what people value. We should remember Keynes' dictum in the same 1933 speech that began this chapter, that some things – perhaps most things – go beyond money. Money may have been a Liberal enthusiasm, used to drive aside the vested interests of the church or the aristocracy. But unless we can see beyond it, then we end up letting money values impoverish. "We are capable of shutting off the sun and the stars because they pay no dividend," wrote Keynes in his speech to the Irish government.[42]

He was right. Liberals must always be able to see beyond the measurements – of money, targets or cost-benefits – to the human realities beneath. As Liberals, we will not subsume the human spirit below counting systems of centralized bureaucracies or massive administrative machines, public or private, Blair-style – to manage politics on our behalf.

## Technology

We addressed in Chapter 3 the impact of technology on our changing culture. Here we address its economic impact and the world of work.

The ubiquitous search engine Google operates a "business model that in less honourable circles is referred to as protection money – i.e if you don't want me to kill you, you have to pay me".[43] So said Axel-Springer's chief executive Mathias Döpfner, accusing Google of misusing its dominant market position. He was warning Europe in particular about the dangers of allowing a handful of technology companies to take over every aspect of our lives. His letter was timely, but seems to have fallen largely on deaf ears, though the European Commission is, at the time of writing, belatedly investigating Google's dominance. This is not a major political issue in the UK, perhaps because of the shockingly muted position of the UK Liberals.

Liberals have traditionally been concerned about controlling the power of business or political monopolies. It is still a major Liberal concern, or it ought to be. Google and Amazon also require political institutions strong enough to break them up if necessary, rather than merely pandering to them and going cap in hand to ask how much local tax they are prepared to pay before they pack up and leave. And it is here that the Liberal case for Europe is at its strongest. No single country, with the possible exceptions of the USA and China, today has the power to match that of such globalised monopolies. They can only be tackled at a supra-national level. It is notable that the current European Competition Commissioner, Margrethe Vestager, has decided to take on these monopolies. She is a Liberal. Her predecessor, a member of Spain's Socialist Workers Party, largely let them slide.

There is a race going on at the moment between the retail or swapping platforms which seek to control increasing proportions of global exchanges and to take a slice of each – from Google and Amazon through to those which seek to sell everything (Tesco) or those which seek to monetize everything (EE or Vodafone) or those who seek to manage every transaction (Visa) – and their potential rivals in the future: the self-managed, co-owned entities which try to challenge them. For example, tiny Hive against Amazon.

You only have to set this out to see the problem. Who is challenging ride-sharing app Uber, for example? There is Lyft and

Juno, but where are the co-owned enterprises that will take them on? Where for example are the childcare co-ops that have kept childcare so civilized and inexpensive in North America? They are successful in Scandinavia, but what about the UK and other parts of Europe?

Even if they did exist – as they will again (childcare co-ops took a battering from inappropriate regulation in the Blair years) – they have on their side that co-ops are more productive than conventional business. They require lower profits. Against them is the sheer scale of their rivals and their ability to drive out opposition or to buy them up, as Amazon bought up their only serious rival in the UK, Book Depository.

There is an alternative scenario, which suggests that we are on the verge of an entirely different kind of economy, driven by the ability of manufacturers to produce at virtually zero-marginal cost. This suggests how the original hopes for a decentralized, personalized economy driven by IT might actually happen, after all. As Paul Mason suggested:

"Almost unnoticed, in the niches and hollows of the market system, whole swaths of economic life are beginning to move to a different rhythm. Parallel currencies, time banks, co-operatives and self-managed spaces have proliferated, barely noticed by the economics profession, and often as a direct result of the shattering of the old structures in the post-2008 crisis..."[44]

The article was taken from Mason's book *Postcapitalism,* arguing that the sharing economy is about to become central to a whole new kind of economics, though the economics mainstream barely sees it at the moment – just as they failed to see the Industrial Revolution until it was on them, or the advent of modern capitalism.

"If I am right," wrote Mason, "the logical focus for supporters of postcapitalism is to build alternatives within the system; to use governmental power in a radical and disruptive way; and to direct all actions towards the transition – not the defence of random elements of the old system."

He warns against sidelining the Left with the politics of protest – "the privatization of healthcare, anti-union laws, fracking – the list goes on" – and urges them to start building the postcapitalist world.

It is difficult to know if he is entirely correct. There are elements where he is missing some explanation – it isn't clear what the motivation will be to produce anything in the postcapitalist world, as Mason sees it. On the other hand, he has to be right about the emerging challenge to the mainstream – and it is a highly practical, pragmatic one, being organized at the moment by thousands (probably no more than that) of people with shirtsleeves rolled up, at local level, experimenting with projects that can build local prosperity.[45]

That has been the central theme of this book: that freewheeling challenge must be possible to the ingrained power patterns, public and private. Indeed, that is what Liberalism is all about. That is what 'free trade' used to mean, in its Liberal sense, though it is clearly not what it has come to mean more recently, which is the feather-bedding of the richest. There is, after all, no point in free movement of capital or technologies or knowledge, without it also being extended to people. In the end, it also will not work. More on that in the next chapter.

Paul Mason and Jeremy Rifkin have set out the key argument for our economic futures and we need to develop institutions which can shape these in such a way that the humane and decentralized future emerges, and the fears of a darker future dominated by the decisions of Big Google or Big Amazon don't come true.[46] Some of the exciting and imaginative experiments going on everywhere will end up being successful. But we lack the institutional capability, maybe even the institutional interest, to take these successes and scale them up quickly. And to do so without losing that which is essential to their success – their bottom-up nature and the fact that they are embedded in the local rather than the global.

## Let us explain ourselves

Some reading this chapter might get the impression that we are putting forward an anti-free trade, anti-globalization, anti-business, anti-European agenda. Nothing could be further from the truth. We believe in all these forces. But we also believe that they should work to provide shared prosperity for all, not for the concentration of power and wealth among the few. We do not advocate a return to protectionism and trade tariffs. That would be a retrograde step.

We also recognize that large, multinational corporations are an essential component of our way of life. Only large entities such as these can build jumbo jets, discover and bring to market new medicines that prolong people's lives and make them better, provide the infrastructure for the transnational financial flows that are essential for thriving economies, and many other activities essential to the modern economy. Our plea is that we recognize that, when taken to excess, everything tends to start breaking down. That unfettered global free trade can lead inexorably to oligopoly and then monopoly. That concentration of power, rising inequality, the creation of a new underclass, the dehumanization of the world of work, the destruction of local economies and the financial insecurity of the new generation (now and when they come to retire) are key economic issues of our time.

We believe that the Liberal approach to tackling these issues lie in the use of government power to liberate the weak by standing up to the strong and by stimulating local economies to sit alongside, and be just as successful as, the globalised economy from which we all benefit. This is the real task of Liberals in Europe and beyond, inside and outside the EU. It is to make that debate mainstream, to carve practical proposals out of it and to make those happen.

Because the Liberals of generations before us, and those to come, demand that this is what we do. It is our destiny to take this argument by the scruff of its neck and to hammer it into some kind of shared understanding of a possible future. How all this translates to a Liberal economics is the subject of our next chapter.

# 5
# Towards a new Liberal economics

*"The first need is to free ourselves of that worst form of contemporary obscurantism which tries to persuade us that what we have done in the recent past was all either wise or unavoidable. We shall not grow wiser before we learn that much that we have done was very foolish."*
**F. A. Hayek, *The Road to Serfdom* (1944)**

It is one of the great ironies of history that, east and west, the liberation of the agricultural slaves and serfs – the people who carried out most of the work in the fields of Russia and eastern Europe and the plantations of the southern US states – happened almost simultaneously.

The slaves were freed by the Emancipation Declaration of Abraham Lincoln in January 1863, though it required another two years to win the Civil War and finish the job. But the Russian serfs were freed from bondage to the land at almost the very same time. The declaration was made in March 1861, to cheers outside the royal palace in St Petersburg, but it also took two years and came to fruition in February 1863, just five weeks after Lincoln promulgated his Emancipation Proclamation.

Both liberations were great victories for the anti-slavery campaigners, more than half a century since the first successes of the campaign against the slave trade, and they came as part of the incomplete flowering of Liberalism on both sides of the Atlantic. But they were also great disappointments for agrarian radicals. Because, in both cases, the slaves and the serfs were catapulted from bondage into poverty.

In the USA, slavery was replaced by peonage and debt bondage. In Russia, the land was valued at three and a half times its market value, and this the impoverished serfs had to pay their former owners over a period of 49 years. For many serfs, even the details of the terms were not agreed for decades. Just as the former slaves had been in the USA, many of the serfs were thrown on the mercies of the money lenders.

In short, it wasn't enough to release the slaves – you had to release them from debt and monopoly and the extractive economic tyranny that replaced it. This was a fundamental flaw in Victorian Liberalism, just as it is a fundamental flaw in Liberalism without an economic edge. The failure of Liberalism to rise to the challenge explains the emergence of socialism as an electable creed in the 1890s.

But Liberalism does have an economic doctrine at its heart, designed to meet precisely this challenge, as we have discussed in earlier chapters. Free trade was intended partly as a response to economic tyranny, set out by David Ricardo and by the political campaigner Richard Cobden. Cobden died in 1865, so he hardly lived to see the aftermath of slave liberation. But he knew all too well that there were such things as economic manacles and that they were just as enslaving as manacles cast in iron. If you just set slaves free, you could bind them just as firmly by forcing them into debt and controlling where they could buy what they needed – just as the Corn Laws forced the English poor to buy bread at inflated prices.

So the original idea of free trade was not a simple license to do whatever you wanted, if you were rich and powerful enough. It was thoroughly aware of Adam Smith's original warning that collusion between entrenched businesses can end in "a conspiracy against the public". It was designed as a means of liberation – so that the small could challenge the big, the poor could challenge the rich with the power of the new approach, the alternative provider, the imaginative, liberating shift.

As we have seen, the economic doctrine at the heart of Liberalism became its own opposite – permission for the rich to ride roughshod over the poor, an apologia for monopoly and an extractive discipline that prevents the all-important challenge from below. Somehow, the global economy has turned in on itself. What started as a way of promoting economic liberation, as Adam Smith envisaged, it has slowly evolved into a tool of enslavement. Not just for the underclass or for the poor in underdeveloped countries, but for all of us – and especially for our children.

This is so especially in disadvantaged cities and countries, where – in the name of free trade – people are locked in a related economic servitude, without the right to trade their way out, or to manage their finances, or to challenge the big banking, energy or grocery semi-monopolies. They are, in short, in precisely the same economic embrace that free trade was originally set out to rescue them from. Part of the revival of Liberalism in the next generation will depend on the ability of Liberals to claw back the original meaning of free trade and to set it to work – not as a licence for economic tyranny but as permission for entrepreneurs from every corner of society, as Anita Roddick put it, to "imagine the world differently".

That means supporting individuals and communities in local

economies all over the UK, including the poorest places, who are making things happen using existing resources. They are operating in the margins, without support or official approval, but they are slowly edging their way towards a new economic diversity. Because of them, and – let's face it, no thanks to many Liberals – the demise of free trade as a radical concept provides an opportunity for its strange rebirth as an underpinning for those local activists who are making things happen, promoting independence and sustainability. It is an idea that could, with recasting, be used to meet local needs.

It hardly needs emphasizing that the real problem goes some way beyond this, though it relates to the same issue – the tyrannical nature of monopoly. A recent article in *Der Speigel* put the issue pretty succinctly.[47] The global economy is no longer working as it should. The banks are not lending, and the huge sums to be distributed by them in the form of quantitative easing simply shore up their balance sheets, the middle classes struggle increasingly to make ends meet – and the poor just struggle. Meanwhile, the handful of those at the top – less than one per cent actually - extract resources in good times and bad.

The idea that the institutions of modern capitalism have become extractive – as institutions have done occasionally in history, with disastrous results – is becoming increasingly accepted. The problem is that there are few agreed solutions, even tentative ones. This is how Michael Sauga puts it in the article, describing the economist Daron Acemoglu:

"He became famous two years ago when he and colleague James Robinson published a deeply researched study on the rise of Western industrial societies. Their central thesis was that the key to their success was not climate or religion, but the development of social institutions that included as many citizens as possible: a market economy that encourages progress and entrepreneurship, and a parliamentary democracy that serves to balance interests.... Extremely well read, Acemoglu can cite dozens of such cases. One is fourteenth century Venice, where a small patrician caste monopolized maritime trade. Another is Egypt under former President Hosni Mubarak, whose officer friends divided up key economic posts among themselves but were complete failures as businessmen. These are what Acemoglu calls 'extractive processes', which lead to economic and social decline. The question today is: Are Western industrial societies currently undergoing a similar process of extraction?"[48]

There is also a parallel with Spain at the height of its imperial power, where the gold poured in, the ability to manufacture withered away and inflation finally overtook the empire.[49] It may be that deflation is the demon that will do for us this time, but we are suffering from the same tyranny of finance over life – of the financial economy over the real one, which undermined Golden Age Spain. It does look increasingly as though the struggling big banks will go through another period of instability, as the big economies begin to unravel again. A new settlement is required – and one that can include people again – and history has a habit of providing these things once the situation is really desperate.

What is more, those moments of reboot seem to happen pretty regularly every forty years or so. The last one was in 1979/80. The one before was the rapid political and economic shift in the UK and USA in 1940/41. Before that, it was the new settlement ushered in by the People's Budget of 1909 and Teddy Roosevelt's busting of Standard Oil, which ended finally in 1911. The big political shift before that came with Gladstone's reforming government in 1868; before that it was the Great Reform Act of 1832. We are not quite overdue for a major reboot, but it is coming and – by this forty-year pattern – it should emerge around 2020. We don't know how it will happen, or what constipated failure to tackle the underlying forces at work will provoke it, but we can be pretty clear already the kind of shape it will be.

And here the *Der Spiegel* article reaches a parallel conclusion, quoting Acemoglu again:

"What is needed, he argues, is a new political alliance that takes a stand against the power of the financial industry and its lobby. He sees the anti-trust movement from the beginning of the last century in the United States as a model. It was a broad coalition from the centre of society and finally achieved its great victory after decades of struggle: the breakup of major corporations like Standard Oil."[50]

It is significant that, once again, the neglected Liberal issue of monopoly power is at the heart of the diagnosis. Nor is it just Liberals who fear they have nothing to say about economics, except to emphasize some minor element of the mainstream or status quo. The whole of the Left prefers to wallow in welfarism or to ignore the creation of prosperity completely, as if the only economic function of the Left was to move money around, and only the Conservative Right could be relied upon to create it in the first place.

In the absence of any new economics, the Left gets increasingly frustrated, and gets cross about language, gets 'offended' by people's jokes – but they retreat from the central issue. In the absence of the traditional critique of monopoly power, Liberals have little to say about economics at all.

Yet we should hardly pretend that the mainstream economy is doing its job, providing the wealth the population needs to flourish. Quite the reverse. We have allowed it to be dominated by the narrow needs of finance, and that has been impoverishing. The identification of finance with the market is part of the underlying problem, and it led to the near collapse of the global market in 2008. This is how the columnist Anatole Kaletsky puts it:

"The explanation centres on an exaggerated and naïve interpretation of economic theory that took to absurd extremes the free-market economic policies applied more pragmatically in the Thatcher-Reagan and Clinton periods. This market fundamentalist approach to economic policy turned a fairly standard, if severe, boom-bust cycle into the greatest financial crisis of all time. More specifically, market fundamentalism was behind the unforced errors of the Bush administration, especially of its treasury secretary, Henry Paulson, that were the proximate cause of financial catastrophe. How could the most powerful and best-resourced government in the world have made so many ruinous mistakes? Much of what went wrong could be attributed to a pernicious interaction between academic economics and political ideology, which magnified each other's faults and biases, like a pair of distorting mirrors. As a result, the classical economics of Adam Smith and David Ricardo were turned into the ludicrously exaggerated doctrines of efficient markets, rational expectations, and monetarist central banking that monopolized economic thinking in governments, regulatory institutions, and financial businesses worldwide."[51]

This is all true. The problem is that it implies for Liberals that the solution is some fatal compromise – the traditional Liberal means of avoiding thinking more fundamentally about economics – when it may be that the market has not been over-emphasized, but has actually been misunderstood. We argued in Chapter 2 that the free market was not originally what it has become – a conservative means for defending the status quo, when it actually was and could still be a means by which the powerless can challenge the powerful, which is how Liberals traditionally understood it.

This fundamental misunderstanding has had serious, impoverishing consequences for us all.

## Let's talk about finance

The reader may have noticed that the last few paragraphs, intended to discuss how a new economy might be built, kept coming back to one recurring theme – finance. Why is an examination of finance important to a discussion about the economy? Because finance and the flow of capital are the life-blood of any capitalist economy. Without an effective financial system an economy is like a body that has all the organs but no blood flowing between them, nourishing them and allowing them to do their job.

There is precious little point in trying to fix the economy without fixing finance. That would be like fixing someone's liver problem if there is not to be any blood flowing to the organ once it is fixed. It will simply shrivel and die. Our economies can therefore never be improved until we have a financial system that is working *for* the larger economy rather than to extract as much value as possible out of it.

In a speech in 2014, Angela Merkel stated that "the danger of another financial crisis is already pre-scripted." She was right, but not because of national budget deficits – the ever-present bug bear of *Ordnungspolitik*. What is much more likely to drive the inevitable recurrence of the next financial crisis is Europe's continued hesitancy in getting to grips with a broken banking and financial system. The banking system was at the centre of the last financial crisis and will likely be at the centre of the next one. Yet, since 2008, the combined efforts of governments, regulators and the banking industry itself have not done enough to tackle the obvious fragility of the system.

Banking reform in Europe has, so far, focused on two main efforts: trying to insulate sovereign debt from bank failure and passing supervision of the large, systemically important banks from national regulators to the European Central Bank (ECB).

The first of these is a chimera. There is little mileage in continuing to pretend that taxpayers can be fully insulated from the failure of large, interconnected, systemically important banks by a combination of building up sufficient reserves and the passing off the costs of failure from governments to the banks' creditors and ordinary savers – the currently fashionable 'bail-in' approach.

First of all, it is all but inconceivable that Eurozone banks will be asked to raise the approximately €1 trillion necessary to make the system resilient in time for the next financial crash. It could also be argued that the more visible and reliable the backstop, the more risk taking it will encourage. Nor is it socially or politically desirable if, as a consequence of bank failure, thousands of ordinary people have their savings wiped out. As the recent episode of Banco Espirito Santo has shown, the sovereign cannot be fully insulated if individual banks are allowed to remain large enough to be systemically important, are allowed to retain integrated operations and, as is inevitable, remain intimately interconnected within the system so that a failure of one threatens many.

If one thing has become clear over the last few years, it is that even the chief executives of the larger banks find themselves unable to have full knowledge of what goes on in the deepest recesses of their complex organizations. The idea that auditors poring over their computers in Frankfurt can gain full insight into all the major banks across the Eurozone is not credible. Such an approach represents blind faith in 'management by spreadsheet' – the technocratic idea that everything can be reduced to rules and numbers. It reflects a mindset that takes an engineering approach to a system that is organic, fluid, dynamic, unpredictable and populated by human beings who will, as human beings do, tend to find ways of dodging around any set of rules. That is, or was, a key Liberal insight and we should not lose sight of it.

The only way to make the system less fragile it to deal with it at a structural level. This can either be done internally by the individual banks or externally through imposition by regulators and, if all else fails, by breaking up the systemically important banks.

One highly experienced banking regulator told us: "Over the years we have tried everything. Nothing has worked." He is right: nothing has worked. But he is wrong that everything has been tried. Meaningful structural remedies are, so far, notable by their absence. Worse, drafting rules that encourage banks to be ever bigger will, at the same time, make the system riskier and make it more costly to do the job that banks are supposed to do: support the real economy. In a conversation with Sir Danny Alexander when he was Chief Secretary to the Treasury in the 2010-2015 coalition, we asked about some key achievements. One of his responses was "we have reformed the banks." Our response was that nothing of the sort had been done. The banks had been further regulated but that is not the same things as reforming the financial system.

While a functioning financial system is essential to a functioning economy, one that fails to function has a disastrous impact on people's lives. *The Economist* put the impact of a non-functioning system like this: "Finance can also terrorize. When bubbles burst and markets crash, plans paved years into the future can be destroyed. As the impact of the crisis of 2008 subsides, leaving its legacy of unemployment and debt, it is worth asking if the right things are being done to support what is good about finance, and to remove what is poisonous."

But before the financial system can be reformed, we need an understanding of a few things. What is the financial system for? Is it achieving those objectives? If not what can be done to reform it and what are the blocks to reform?

## *What is the financial system for?*

The financial services industry has a core social function – that of ensuring that capital flows smoothly to all the important parts of an enterprise society at minimum frictional cost. This will enable investment, growth and financial security for all. The industry also has a key role in risk intermediation. Unfortunately, the financial services industry is not currently performing these functions effectively and, in its current form, may not be able to go back to performing them adequately. Why?

The first reason is that the financial services industry has become plagued by the disease that has affected many other sectors. It has lost sight of its core social purpose and instead become focused exclusively on how to maximize its own profits. Rather than seeing profit as being the consequence of effectively and efficiently fulfilling its social function, profit maximization has itself become the sole purpose for the existence of many financial services firms. As a result, products and services are designed and sold because they make the firms involved money, even if such products destroy both financial and social value for others. Hence we have tax arbitrage products that destroy social value, re-packaging and securitization of sub-prime mortgages that led to the financial crash, a global financial system that still carries has some $550 trillion in outstanding derivatives contracts with a risk profile that is largely unknown, and so on.

Next, we have a system that encourages firms to take extreme risks. Again, this is because the upside of risk flows to the firms themselves while the downside is underwritten by others – mainly the public purse. This has been the case for as long an anyone can remember.

Then we have the issue of size, and oligopoly that has been a recurrent theme in this book. Because of the concentration of the sector and the essential nature of the services that it provides, oligopolistic firms can extract more value out of the economy than they would be able to in a functioning, truly competitive market. As such, rather than minimizing the frictional costs of finance, they are maximized to the greatest extent possible.

Next we have the complex interconnectedness of the financial system that we mentioned earlier where the failure of one threatens to bring down the whole system.

Then we have the financialization of the real economy. What does this mean? It means that all value that is exchanged becomes reduced to a financial instrument that can be traded. Or, as Greta Krippner of the University of Michigan puts it, a "pattern of accumulation in which profit making occurs increasingly through financial channels rather than through trade and commodity production". Trading of financial instruments then becomes a money-making activity, with the underlying value that was created in the real economy largely becoming irrelevant.

The prime example of this process is the trading of company shares on the stock market. The value of the stock market is, today, largely driven by the trading of shares and retains very little connection to the actual performance of the companies whose shares are being traded. This leads to all sorts of behaviour that damages the real economy. It leads companies – and particularly those where senior executive compensation is tied to stock price performance – to prioritize financial engineering that pushes up their stock price over investment in the patient growth of their business. Also, when policy-makers such as central banks use 'the markets' as a guide to policy, they mean the financial markets which are a poor guide to the performance of the real economy.

Finally, we have the inexorable rise of computer mediated trading where algorithms are built into the system to react instantly to market movements. The net result of this is that every finance house reacts instantly and largely uniformly to market signals. The consequence is that at the first sign of market instability or increased risk, all the computers instantly kick in and sell what the algorithms deem to be too risky. A market wobble can thereby be instantly converted into a market crash.

But none of this is a problem, some would say. Because markets are efficient and, in ways that we cannot really hope to understand will end up allocating capital efficiently. Any kind of government or regulatory intervention will only make things worse. That is the looking glass world of market fundamentalists and it explains why finance has ended up destroying the real economy rather than building it up.

## The myth of efficient markets

One of the peculiarities of the financial world over the past two decades or more, which has drawn even more of the working population into its grip, has been the recruitment of physicists and mathematicians into the exclusive world of trading and electronic markets – the growing belief that there were patterns to be recognized in the markets if only you could see them. One of the British pioneers of that idea has been Paul Woolley, who now runs his own think tank in London and Toulouse dedicated to explaining why the financial markets have been so disastrous to the economy of the world, and especially in the UK, where they have developed almost more than anywhere else.

He has grown deeply sceptical of the ability of finance to allocate resources effectively – which is the job description of financial services, and the idea which has driven their extraordinary growth during the past generation.

Part of the building blocks of the dysfunctional system is the way economic doctrine fails to describe the real world, especially around the economic doctrine known as the Efficient Market Hypothesis. Promulgated by the Chicago economist Eugene Fama and his colleagues in 1970, it suggested that market prices were always right. They took all the available information and computed the correct price. The Hypothesis lay behind the extraordinary growth in financial trading since then, and it remains the justification for the vast rewards of the traders. They are paid so well, or so they say, because they are efficiently producing accurate prices.

But there was a peculiar contradiction about the Efficient Market Hypothesis: it meant that there could not be any price anomalies for traders to exploit for a bargain. Yet clearly that was what traders thought they were doing. Woolley found that, in practice, stock prices tended to overshoot. They carry on going up beyond what ought to be the top of the market, just as momentum tends to take them down further than they should go at the bottom. Here was a potential key to unlock the puzzle, and it was the central flaw to the Efficient Market Hypothesis on which everything else was based.

Woolley argued that, despite conventional wisdom, the markets are not actually efficient after all. The prices are not accurate. The traders are not fairly recompensed as efficient organizers, sorting resources to their most productive uses. They are overpaid *rentiers* presiding over what he calls a 'wobbling blancmange of mispricing'. And every time they sort, whether the bet wins or loses – and the fee structure encourages them to trade faster and faster – they carve another slice for themselves. If financial markets are dysfunctional, it actually increases demand for services, and because the investors were so inefficient at providing the returns people might expect, they had to invest more often and more frenetically. The huge scale of the financial sector was a testimony to its failure, as it sucked in the resources that ought to have been providing the rest of us with productive, lucrative activity.[52]

The result is the over emphasis of speculative assets over productive ones. Banking assets were worth about half of UK GDP when we were in school (1970); now they are worth six times UK GDP. Even the biggest four UK banks are worth three times UK GDP, as financial services and financial trading slowly push out the productive economy like the cuckoo in the nest.

The cult of the heroic banker has gone hand in hand with the cult of the heroic CEO. The banker John Pierpont Morgan, founder of JP Morgan, used to say that nobody at the top of a company should earn more than twenty times those at the bottom (a bottom-to-top ratio of 1:20). That was widely understood by many companies for most of the twentieth century. The Royal Navy, which was sensitive about its own equitable culture, especially after the embarrassment of the Invergordon Mutiny against pay cuts in 1931, had for many years a ratio of lowest to highest of 1:8.

But we have forgotten these guidelines, and the resulting divisions have been corrosive to the middle classes as well as everyone else. Those who work their way up to be a Royal Navy captain, or a local solicitor or head teacher, or a range of other professionals which provided the backbone to the middle classes, are not just priced out of the old benefits of middle-class life – from homes to private education – they are also undermined by the sheer scale of the pay packets of those in the financial elite. It doesn't matter how much they earn, there will still be someone out there who will make their efforts, their expertise and their salary look puny.

"Why on earth should finance be the biggest and most highly paid industry when it is just a utility, like sewage or gas?" Paul Woolley asked the *New Yorker* in 2010.[53] "It is like a cancer that is growing to infinite size until it takes over an entire body." And in these circumstances you can understand a situation where the money that changes hands in speculation every day dwarfs the money involved in real production, where banking arms deliberately set out to ruin small businesses in order to earn the fees from administering their exhausted carcasses, and where whole nations are handed over to the European bankers for the good of all.

It is easy to point the finger but, actually, Liberals need to take their share of the blame. They failed to understand that Milton Friedman's neoliberalism had little in common with F. A. Hayek's new Liberalism, and was in fact a complete reversal of the Liberal tradition (see Chapter 2). They failed to hold on to their central belief in the importance of policing monopoly and abuse of market positions.

## What is to be done?

Let's go back to Anatole Kaletsky, who is not alone in blaming the current economic impasse on a fundamentalist alliance between ivory-tower policy-makers and ivory-towered academics, peddling an idea that the narrowest form of economic analysis could solve any conundrum. This is what he wrote in his book *Capitalism 4.0:*

> "Most serious political philosophers, sociologists, and economic historians have long realized that the opposite is true. Any society driven purely by market incentives will fail catastrophically, in economic as well as political terms. The freest, most incentive-driven market economies in the world are not the United States or Hong Kong or even tax havens such as the Cayman Islands but failed states and gangster societies such as Somalia, Congo, and Afghanistan..."[54]

There is certainly a problem with market fundamentalism, and – as we have seen – a learned helplessness about new thinking in the policy-making world. But for Liberals, this isn't enough. To blame it all on pushing the idea of the market in a fundamentalist way makes them look as if they are advocating some kind of compromise again, whereas the Liberal critique potentially goes far deeper than that. The Liberal approach to economics has to now be about reconnecting people with the economy, to make sure they are not wrenched from it as they are currently being by monopolists and policy-makers with a deterministic commitment to giantism.

How do we reconnect finance to the real economy and also get back to the idea that the economy is about people, not just about numbers? This is a mammoth task. Here we focus on just two aspects – reforming finance and creating shaping new institutions capable of supporting local economies and Liberal entrepreneurs, people able and willing to make things happen.

*Reforming Finance*
The first element that is essential in reforming finance is finding ways of moving away from the overwhelming market power of the incumbents. Unfortunately, this has not been a priority for most regulators. Instead, they seem to have accepted that retaining big, global banks is the only way forward and have focused their efforts on making them more resilient to financial shocks. Whether their efforts in building resilience have been successful we shall see when the next crash comes. But we reject the notion that the current industry structure is the only viable one.

There are a number of options available for moving away from the current oligopolistic structure. The first is, clearly to inject more competition – especially at local level – an issue that we will come back to in the next section. But here we have a problem since the massive increase in banking regulation over the last six years has made it more difficult for smaller challengers to enter the market. Regulators, fearful of unknown consequences, seem unwilling to relax the requirements for new entrants. We also suspect that many regulators do not really want to have to deal with regulating hundreds of banks so the failure of new entrants is, to some degree, welcome for them however unwelcome it is for the country and its people.

The reluctance of regulators to encourage new market entrants is illustrated by what happened in the UK some years ago. Parliamentarians asked the regulator why they were not issuing new banking licences. The response was that they had had no applications to set up new banks. On further investigation, it turned out that a number of new applications had been put forward but, in every single case, the applicants had been contacted privately by the regulators and told that there may be some issues with the application so the applicant might prefer to withdraw it rather than have the spectre of a public rejection hanging over him. Applications were duly withdrawn allowing regulators to claim that no banking licences had in fact been withheld.

This aspect of the regulation issue has since been resolved and new challenger banks are emerging. But this does highlight the issues of the incentive systems under which regulators operate.

Many are placing their faith in the rise of fintech companies, another sector that is generating regulatory angst. This may hold promise but it is far too early to say whether fintech will be able to grow sufficiently to service the real economy effectively. And it is also not clear whether this new sector will provide the social value that is needed from the finance sector, or whether it will also become trapped in the *rentier* culture so characteristic of the financial services sector.

In a dysfunctional market such as this, it would be perfectly legitimate to introduce competition through the use of public entities. The setting up of the Green Investment Bank and the Business Bank in the UK are such examples. There is no reason why more financial services entities with a clear mission to serve the real economy could not be set up by the government. The standard riposte that such an approach would lead to market distortion can hardly be put forward when 'distortion' hardly starts to describe the utter dysfunction of the current market structure.

Breaking up the systemically important banks is an option that is always on the table but is never picked up. Maybe because of the lobbying power of the industry. Maybe because policy-makers believe the narrative that "we have to have globally competitive banks" – even if nobody else believes that line any more. Maybe because of the practical difficulties in implementation. The seemingly simple process of spinning off Williams and Glyn's from the Royal Bank of Scotland has now been abandoned because management could not find a way of separating the new bank's IT infrastructure – even after spending over £1bn of the public's money trying to do so. In the UK, even the separation of retail banking from investment banking has been fudged and diluted.

Finally, there is the option of treating large parts of the banking system as public utilities and regulating them as such. In an era of prolonged low interest rates, banking profits are, in any case, all but evaporating. Regulating banks as utilities with 'guaranteed' profits may, in a few years' time not seem like such a bad option for some. Part of this might involved a UK version of the highly successful Community Reinvestment Act in the USA which insists that, where banks are unable to lend money to their own customers, they fund new community level banks which can (see below).

These are a few of the available options and there are doubtless many more. But what is clear to any Liberal is that it is impossible to create a Liberal economy with the current structure of finance. Structural remedies will therefore become essential – whatever they might end up looking like.

## Local institutions

Localism and subsidiarity have been recurring themes in this book and they are fundamental to building a Liberal economy. What are the signs, if any, that local economies are able to emerge?

Local banks, a national enterprise bank and co-operative public service micro-enterprises are not unknown in the UK. But they either support or depend on local financial institutions which know and understand the local market. In the UK we lack these services, partly because of historic legacies to do with the way banks have been regulated in the UK – but also because we have lost our own tradition of economic innovation at local level.

Yet, even in the UK, there is an ultra-local economics sector emerging. It is diverse and small-scale, and does not see or describe itself in those terms, but it is there. It emerges from the bundle of ideas around regeneration that is given any of the following labels: asset-based economics, sustainable local economics, community-based economics, resilient local economics, using local resources to develop 'diversity, flexibility and increasing capacity'. It is an immensely practical approach to economics, which involves the assets that places have to hand, including their own people and their knowhow and enthusiasms.[55]

Two pieces of academic research support this as a prediction. In particular, the *Harvard Business Review* research in 2010 which concluded that "more small firms means more jobs. Our research shows that regional economic growth is highly correlated with the presence of many small, entrepreneurial employers—not a few big ones." it says.[56] In 2012, the journal *Economic Development Quarterly* confirmed these findings:

"Economic growth models that control for other relevant factors reveal a positive relationship between density of locally owned firms and per capita income growth, but only for small (10-99 employees) firms, whereas the density of large (more than 500 workers) firms not owned locally has a negative effect."[57]

There is a sense in which this is where Liberal economics emerged. When the first Liberal mayor of Birmingham, Joseph Chamberlain, addressed councillors in the 1870s, he told them to 'be more expensive'. This hardly a phrase you hear much these days, partly because its meaning has changed: he probably meant 'more ambitious'. And Chamberlain was nothing if not ambitious. He had just seized control of a city that was in a desperate state, with poisoned rivers, occasional water supplies, and hideous poverty. He had also seized it from a group of independent councillors who met regularly in a pub called The Woodman, and who prided themselves on their ability to avoid spending any money. They called themselves 'The Economists'.

In this respect, Chamberlain is in some ways a very modern hero. He revived Britain's second city, paved it, lit its streets, and infused it with enormous pride, and built parks and galleries and concert halls. He did so, not by begging for central government subsidies or from Chinese investment, but from using the assets at his disposal – the foul water, the money flowing through, the local people. Chamberlain municipalized the water and gas supply and used the profits to reshape the city and fund the arts.

Now, fourteen decades later, we may be back to this kind of pattern. The investment is usually not forthcoming and the central government tap has run dry, rightly or wrongly. We could wait around until we control the tap again, but there are more fundamental reasons why it has run dry which will make it more difficult to turn.

Local government is going to have to rediscover the entrepreneurial skills of using what assets lie before them. Unfortunately, they have been constrained over the past two generations by two generally accepted truths that have both proved to be completely wrong. One, that the economic levers are all in Whitehall, and economic decisions are supposed to be made there; two, that all they can do to is to beg for government handouts or major corporate investment.

The absolute necessity for Liberals to be more practical in their approach to economics is most obvious here – the need to overthrow these twin assumptions. And at its heart is an old idea: that where people are gathered together, the basic necessities for growing an effective economy ought to be available. People have needs, skills and time; what they lack is the business support to bring these elements together. So a progressive economic policy would look to provide the framework for economies at any level to thrive by exploiting the assets they have at their disposal.

The economic techniques for growing an effective economy

have long since been forgotten and have not just atrophied – they have been undermined by the monopolies and semi-monopolies that have been allowed to dominate so many local economies, from groceries to energy and refuse collection. But there is here the outline of a very practical agenda for a new Liberal economics – economic devolution, local lending institutions to support local enterprise, and a major programme of monopoly-busting.

This emerging *ultra-local* economics sector is about repatriating some economic activity, shortening supply chains, reducing carbon footprints and allowing the local economy to service more of its own demand – and, by doing so, to soak up the spare capacity in struggling areas. And it is also already remarkably clear about what it believes, broadly that there are assets in communities: knowledge, skills, unused resources, land and buildings and money flows that can be harnessed to support local economic development.

This ultra-micro approach is based on the following principles that, even in the most distressed areas:

- There is money in *all* communities, but not nearly enough institutions invest locally and those which do exist are often too risk averse to grow local markets.
- There are assets in *all* communities – knowledge, skills, resources, land and buildings – that might be harnessed to support local economic development, despite the lack of skills and capital.
- There is money flowing through *all* local economies but, when there are few local enterprises and supply chains, it tends to flow straight out again.
- There is a sense of place at local level, where many of the

economic levers belong.

The argument against an approach like this is that it is protectionist. That is a misreading. The point is to provide a freer market, not by putting up barriers but by empowering competitors – by creating choice, not limiting it.

The most urgent requirement here is local lending institutions. The big banks have over 80 per cent market share but are no longer geared up for the kind of local lending that is needed, and local financial support to entrepreneurs. Their regional structures do not allow them to use the local information they need to assess risk. Most of the emerging local banks, like Cambridge & Counties, are not intending to accept deposits. There are exceptions to this, and there are start-ups that are using new technology or P2P systems, but again they lack the local knowledge they need. There are also other unusual or more maverick solutions, like the heroic Bank on Dave in Burnley.

As well as these, the Lib Dems in government wrestled with the system to start the previously mentioned Green Investment Bank, which specializes in loans for green infrastructure, the Big Society Bank (specializing in social enterprise lending), and the new Business Bank. But welcome though these are, they don't amount to a solution to the basic problem. The UK still suffers from the debilitating lack of effective local banks and from a lending infrastructure that is no longer designed to encourage enterprise. This is not possible without the infrastructure to price local risk effectively.

For that reason, if no other, it matters that just 3 per cent of banks are local in the UK, compared to 34 per cent in the USA, 33 per cent in Germany and 44 per cent in Japan.[58] This puts the UK at an important disadvantage against competitor nations.

Studies in Italy and Germany found that co-operative and savings banks help reduce the drain of capital from urban centres and foster regional equality because of their ability to lend to SMEs.[59] It is also important that, although they accounted for one fifth of the European banking market, co-operative banks suffered only 8 per cent of total losses incurred during the financial crisis.[60]

The mismatch of investment is staggeringly inefficient in the UK. Like the USA, the UK's value added earning figures come about half from big companies and half from SMEs. But only about 11 per cent of the investment goes to SMEs. You might argue, of course, that they don't need the kind of investment that big companies do, and that's true. But so much of our national wealth, ingenuity, time and effort goes into supporting big companies, and often at the expense of SMEs, which – as the research shows – has only a marginal effect on local prosperity.

*The supply of money*
One of the most peculiar and unnerving elements of the structural design of the economy is the way that, even in the richest parts of the world, the middle classes – even those on relatively high salaries – are unable to afford a civilized life without state subsidy of student fees, home ownership, transport and mortgage relief. Ministers failed to understand that, if you subsidize home ownership, the prices would rise. Consequently, home ownership is now impossible unless both partners work full-time and, in London at least, in financial services.

There is a parallel here with the eurozone. There, the outlying nations are forced into an indebted relationship with Germany and the ECB because the interest rates of the single currency are set to support the centre (see Chapter 4). It is the same in the UK, where interest rates suit London – but would cause inflation there if they were set to suit the relatively impoverished cities of the north. As a result, governments need to stimulate demand by creating money in a convoluted way through quantitative easing, which – because of the way it is organized – goes straight into the banks, fuelling bankers bonuses, London house prices and the prices of financial assets like stock prices. Quantitative Easing ends up enriching the already wealthy and further impoverishing the poor while little if any of the newly created liquidity ends up reaching the real economy.

This is another vital area where Liberals are destined to intervene. If the flow of money is now impossible to sustain civilized life, then it needs to be created in a more effective way – not in the form of mortgage lending, as most of the money in circulation in the UK now starts its life, but created by the Bank of England under democratic control and spent into circulation in productive investment.[61]

**

The bottom line is this. The UK has the most extraordinary record of innovation. It has imaginative and possibly even an increasingly entrepreneurial population. They are let down by the antiquated and centralized banking system, which fuels property bubbles at the expense of real enterprise, unbalancing the economy and encouraging a ruinous boom-bust cycle.

Worse, we also have an education system that still ignores the practical, entrepreneurial intelligences at the expense of the purely academic. That is what happens when the Liberal understanding and the Liberal angle are excluded from education policy for too long (see Chapter 8).

## Liberalism as an entrepreneurial force

For the past century or so, business has occupied a similar niche in the political pantheon. It has supported the status quo. It has been a voice for conservatism, allied to conservative parties, cheer-leading conservative victories. But something is happening that has upset that rule: the major energy of entrepreneurial business has shifted behind radical change.

This is a revolution that has only just begun. It can hardly apply to all business people, and many will not change their vote as a result of it. But the key point is that many of them are doing so, because business is emerging again – as it once was – as a radical force in the way that the future is being shaped.

It is happening paradoxically when the reputation of business has been at an absolute nadir, almost as low as the reputation of politicians. It is a shift driven by self-interest, of course, but it is more than self-interest. It is based on the rising frustrations of business with the extreme conservatism of the UK establishment and administrative machinery.

It is so particularly of business people in three areas. They are increasingly outward-looking, internationalist, advocates of open borders, free travel and exchange and fresh ideas, when conservatism around the world is at the very least divided on the issue. They are no longer supporting the status quo in quite the same way. Quite the reverse, they are backing long-term thinking against short-termism, vocational skills not just academic ones, and new institutions which can achieve what the old ones have failed to do. They are also overwhelmingly in favour of a new skills agenda which puts confidence, resilience and creativity at the heart of a new relationship between schools and business, when the UK establishment has traditionally failed to look beyond academic elitism.

These three are significant politically because all three are based on a practical ideology which is politically Liberal. In fact, business may now be returning to its original Liberal roots.

There are exceptions to this. Not all business is enlightened and forward-looking in the way we describe. Short-termism has been corrosive of strategic and moral purpose. Also the shift is not yet reflected in the conventional business lobby groups, which tend to follow the lead of their biggest multinational members – assuming, quite wrongly, that they speak for all business. There have also been misunderstandings about enterprise, traditionally something which politicians regard purely through the lens of money – as if that was the only motivating factor. Of course, entrepreneurs are motivated by money – who isn't? But they are also motivated, as we suggested above, by their ability to imagine the world differently.

For most of the nineteenth century, business instinctively supported the radical force in UK politics. It was Liberal then, just as it is increasingly Liberal now. But then, Liberals and Conservatives see business differently. Conservatism regards business as supporting the status quo. For Liberals, business has always been about change. It has always involved allowing new ideas to challenge old ones, for new innovations to challenge the entrenched ways of doing things. It has always meant that the small should be allowed to challenge the big. Conventional wisdom has to be challengeable, by ideas or entrepreneurs, which is why – as Karl Popper put it – open societies tend to be more adaptable than closed ones (see Chapter 1).

Conservatism wants business to achieve some sort of stability. Liberalism wants them to be resilient, aware that change comes from everywhere and is rarely predictable. It all comes down to a question of what business is for. It feeds people, nurtures people, provides then with what they need and want. It pays people – or it should – the basic money they need to live. But it isn't static: it doesn't keep still, and it is that entrepreneurial energy which makes all the difference to a Liberal view of business.

Business which underpins the status quo wants schools which turn out potential employees who can read, write and do basic maths. Business which imagines the world differently needs that too, but something much more – they need potential employees who are creative, imaginative and able to make things happen. They need people who can start their own enterprise at some point in their lives. Not everyone will want to do that, but – even if they never do – businesses increasingly want problem solvers, question askers and creative thinkers. They don't want people who can just do what they are told; they want people who can think and do for themselves.

That is why the entrepreneurial power of business tends to scare traditional government and unnerves the big political parties. It involves thinking differently, seeing the world differently, doing things differently, when government is overwhelmingly concerned with compliance. That is the meaning of Liberal business.

We have been through nearly a century where the interaction between business and the state has been reduced to a stale, uni-dimensional discussion. More government versus less government, more regulation versus less regulation, the rights of business versus the rights of the worker, foreigners versus locals. It is an agenda that is outdated, divisive and unproductive. It fails to create the radical manifesto that we need to create a flourishing enterprise society that benefits everyone. Yet both Labour and the Conservatives seem wedded to this stale agenda. Conservatives promise to be 'on the side of business' by maintaining the status quo and cutting public services (on which business is also dependent). Labour seems intent on shackling business and small business in particular. Neither is in tune with the emerging radical force in today's business world.

A radical economics manifesto would set out plans to build an education system that produces entrepreneurs. It would train people to think differently, and to make things happen. It would shift the snobbish and ineffective imbalance in our universities and training systems which has traditionally rewarded the academic and ignored the creative, the vocational and the humanities – the subjects that are concerned with how we live as a functioning society. It would revitalize the digital potential of the nation, and it would build banks that were fit for purpose.

Above all, it would shift the mindset of the nation to emphasize enterprise, problem solving, creativity, self-help, reasonable risk and positive change. A mindset that sees change as an opportunity to be encouraged rather than threat to be avoided. In other words, a mindset that is open and Liberal rather than closed and conservative, or stuck in the class warfare rhetoric of the last century. It would ask what kind of society, and what kind of schools, would produce entrepreneurs – and would fearlessly pursue the ideas that emerged.

That is a pretty fundamental change. Imagine that politics began to grasp what it means to be an entrepreneur, and began to model government around the idea of fast-moving, creative and strategic thinking. Imagine that, instead of modelling themselves on huge bureaucracies or databases, or great military machines, the departments of state could understand themselves and their individual staff as creative, enterprising, capable and fast. Imagine that, instead of modelling themselves on the old business megaliths of the past, they might begin to learn the lessons of social and business entrepreneurs – determined to make a difference.[62]

For inspiration, Britain can look at its performance in the last two Olympic Games. There is little doubt that the country punched above its weight. That was the result of adequate funding (the equivalent of good finance for business), working to generate skills and enthusiasm starting in the schools, the ability to bring together the best of British skills in technology, engineering and all the other disciplines from nutrition to fitness training, good organization, and a determination to succeed. If Britain can do it in sports, what are the barriers to doing the same across the world of enterprise? It is notable that in interview after interview during the Rio games, sporting leaders had one message: we can continue to be successful because we have the skills and the abilities, but whatever you do don't stop the funding.

Which brings us back to where we started this chapter – without finance reform the economy is unable to succeed.

**

We are not naive enough to believe that simple exhortations to innovate and launch enterprises to underpin life are enough to shift the structural problems of a global economy dedicated to creating billionaires. But the idea that entrepreneurs – interpreted differently – are at the heart of a powerful new economics is central to Liberal thinking. It is also a potential building block for the devolution of some economic levers, and the heart of a very practical agenda for a new Liberal economics: economic devolution, local lending institutions, creativity in schools, and a major programme of monopoly-busting.

The world is entering a period when mainstream multinational business, with its managerial and technocratic worldview, has lost its tentative licence to operate – because it is no longer able, in the face of widespread technological change, to employ and support the majority of the world in civilized lives. In those circumstances, Liberals need to find new ways that we can support people to lead lives that support a tolerant, open society, and to create the enterprises that will make a major difference. That debate has not yet taken place, but some have suggested that we might need to provide people with the basic income they need, as of right, and do it through a form of quantitative easing that is different from that which is currently in place – and to avoid inflation by making the economy more equal and by preventing the mainstream banks from creating money in the old way.

It seems likely that it will involve new kinds of money that circulate for different purposes and in different ways. It also seems likely to include major anti-monopoly legislation to unleash the entrepreneurial revolution we need.

In short, we have been released from the bonds of slavery by nineteenth century Liberalism, but we have not yet been released from the encroaching bonds of economic peonage. That is a task for which twenty-first century Liberalism was born for, if it can get to grips with the challenge.

# 6

# Abolishing the environment ministries

*Nature's bequest gives nothing, but doth lend,*
*And being frank she lends to those are free:*
*Then, beauteous niggard, why dost thou abuse*
*The bounteous largess given thee to give?*
*Profitless usurer, why dost thou use*
*So great a sum of sums, yet canst not live?*
**William Shakespeare, Sonnet Number IV**

We should start by abolishing all ministries of the environment.

This may sound like a strange opening. It does, however, get to the crux of one of the most important issues related to environmental politics – environmental issues do not stand alone, they are inextricably intertwined with broad economic and social considerations. Putting environmental considerations in a box – separate ministries, separate chapters as in this book, separate sections in political manifestos, and so forth – may be organizationally convenient, but it simply reinforces the impression that environmental issues need to be tackled separately from 'more important' issues such as the economy, human health and well being, inequality and all else.

We use 'environment' here in its original meaning: the

aggregate of things, conditions or influences that surround us. In other words, all that is around us that affects life, well-being and prosperity (however defined). Rather than being separate, environmental considerations are therefore crucial components of all that we do. In that spirit, we don't need ministries for the environment that try to push their own narrowly defined 'green' policies often in conflict with all other ministries. Rather than having separate environmental policy, what we need is for environmental considerations to be routinely embedded in every ministry, every government department and every part of government policy.

What the rise in the environmental debate over the last several decades has done is to provide us with the opportunity to look at the structures and functions of our economies, societies and institutions from a different perspective. As such, it has the potential to enrich the debate while providing us with a different viewing platform from which we can survey our social and economic structures. A different outlook that, well used, can help us re-imagine the world. Yet, to achieve all this we need to abandon the habit of green activism – a mindset that extracts environmental considerations from their wider context and places them front and centre in the policy debate – often believing that all other considerations should be subordinated to the environmental perspective. In that similar vein, we don't need green political parties that likewise have a unifocal environmental perspective, with other policies tagged on in an attempt to make them seem something other than single issue activist organizations. Rather, we need political parties that have rounded and comprehensive platforms every part of which explicitly includes environmental considerations in all aspects of policy.

Politically, environmental considerations have long been associated in voters' minds with left-leaning politics. Many environmental activists originate on the left of the political spectrum. A number mesh their concern for the environment with a visceral dislike of a Liberal, market system they would prefer to overthrow. Proposed policy approaches often involve all pervasive statism. As one senior UK Liberal politician put it: "I am fully in support of protecting and restoring our environment. My problem is that the green lobby's approaches for getting there are profoundly illiberal." This has put environmental issues firmly in the politics of the unreasonable left, thereby alienating and losing the support of the vast swathe of the population that is in the political centre or leans to the right.

Such a positioning has also opened the way for many parties of the right to dismiss a green political ideology that they portray as detached from economic and practical reality. This political positioning enables leaders like David Cameron to win plaudits for stripping policy bare of any environmental considerations – what he came to call 'green crap' – only a few short years after he promised that any government he led would be 'the greenest government ever.' Those interested in environmental issues may bemoan, or even despair at, such a turn. But they might also do well to reflect whether it might be their own earnest but myopic political positioning that opened up the opportunity.

The reality of the twenty-first century is that there is increasing voter interest – especially among the young – in environmental issues and their impact on people's health and well-being as well as the sustainability of our economies. Yet, in all countries, such interest still remains subordinate to other considerations – jobs, security, access to health care and education, and many others. In spite of decades of effort, and multi-millions spent, by the environmental movement in trying to lift environmental considerations higher in voters' priorities, these efforts have had only limited success. It could be argued that some of these efforts may even have been counter-productive. Whether one agrees with it or not, a strong perception has been created among a significant proportion of citizens that environmental policy works directly against their economic and other interests. Hence Cameron's ability to U-turn not only with impunity but to widespread applause. Environmentalists have tried to finesse this issue by portraying the utopia of a green economy, but this has so far been largely an incoherent abstraction full of internal contradictions and too far removed from everyday practical reality to have significant political or popular resonance.

Our contention in this chapter is that continuing to address environmental issues within their own separate silo will remain counter-productive. Similarly the longer environmental issues keep being associated in people's minds with militant activism originating in the political left, the easier it is for opponents to ridicule and marginalize them.

Might the situation change? The number of organizations engaged in, at best unco-ordinated, at worst conflicting, environmental activism continues to grow. Single issue activism is their stock in trade, and they will continue to ply that trade whether or not it is politically effective or counter-productive. For change to materialize, it may need to be driven by political parties as much as activists.

## The environment is not about nature

As Corrado Poli puts it in his book *Environmental Politics,* environment "concerns both human built artefacts and that which interacts with humans."[63] Conflating environment with nature and focusing heavily on the latter simply tends to drive yet more wedges, and create more conflict, between what is perceived to be in the human interest and the interest of nature, however one might choose to define such an ambiguous, socially constructed term that has an ever-changing cultural meaning. It also furthers the tendency to equate 'environment' narrowly with questions related to natural ecosystems, species extinction, climate change, the old tedious and largely fruitless debates around 'deep' *versus* 'shallow' ecology, and so forth.

While this may reflect the origins of the environmentalist movement, its co-option by eco-warriors who often originate from the natural sciences, and the very origin of the language that equates 'environment' with 'green', it results in a narrow and largely unhelpful focus that pits the human against the non-human.

In that spirit, this chapter is not structured around 'environmental issues' or 'green policy.' Instead, we address some of the broad social and economic issues of our time and examine their interaction with the conditions that surround us and on which we depend for our wellbeing. Consider this chapter an extension of our other chapters with some of the same issues being looked at from a different perspective. We do not engage with issues relating to environmental remediation – landscape restoration, species recovery, and so forth. Important as these initiatives are, they are remedies for the environmental damage that has been wreaked. They are addressing the symptoms rather than the cause.

As the biologist E. O. Wilson put it in a *New York Times*

opinion piece: "The global conservation movement is like a surgeon in an emergency room treating an accident victim: He has stopped the bleeding by half. Congratulations, we might say – even though the patient will be dead by morning."[64]

In this chapter, we focus our attention on the root causes of environmental degradation and how we might address those. Without action to address these root causes, remediation becomes a losing battle.

We would also encourage politicians to abandon the term 'green' when they are talking about environmental politics and policy. While a green flag may be a useful rallying point for people who are already converted, it is also polarizing, has the unhelpfully narrow connotations that we describe above and has grown to be a divisive term incapable of creating a broad enough coalition of interests to achieve the system changes we need so badly.

The narrow green agenda has also blinded mainstream political parties to the broad reality of what people need. The impoverished business of focus group or opinion poll policy-making makes them categorize environmental politics, for example, as entirely different from people's concerns about health. Green issues tend to score low, but health issues tend to score high – people are highly motivated by the need to protect their own and their children's health from air pollution, pesticides or radiation. But the political parties characterize this differently, and Liberal politicians often miss the connections between these issues and the fundamental source of Liberalism – people's demand for independence from the corrosive effects of these debilitating pollutants on their children's health.

In the end, pollution undermines people's freedom to live healthy, independent lives. These are powerful motivators but – by categorizing green issues separately – mainstream parties have failed to exploit them for change.

Finally, we need to overcome the conflict and confusion that arises from the politics of 'green' in Liberal circles. Many argue that the green agenda is a natural space for Liberal parties. This perspective tends to emerge from narrow electoral considerations – there are a number of voters out there who care about environmental issues and Liberal parties can capture these votes by having an explicitly green shade to their political platforms. Other Liberals are, on the other hand, put off by the green agenda because they regard some policy proposals put forward by environmental activists as fundamentally illiberal – policies focused on coercive approaches that control people's lives even, as we outlined in Chapter 2, at the cost of abandoning democratic principles in the interests of the greater green good. These conflicts disappear if we abandon the idea of a green agenda and focus, as we suggest here, on embedding broad environmental considerations as an integral part of the democratic policy making process focused on Liberal principles.

## About sustainability

An academic friend recently said that, in order to win grants these days, applications somehow need to contain two words "inter-disciplinary" and "sustainability." While this may simply reflect current fashion, it might just happen to be a good fashion. We argue here that inter-disciplinarity and sustainability are intimately inter-connected. Let us start by talking about sustainability. We will address inter-disciplinarity later in our chapter on education.

What is sustainability? What does the word mean? Does it have cultural meaning? We would argue that sustainability is – to date – somewhat meaningless. We also consider that its very meaninglessness is its biggest strength.

Sustainability is possibly the one word in the environmental vocabulary that can unite rather than divide. Talk about climate change, conservation, even the very word environment and you have a fight on your hands. Meaningful engagement has become impossible as factions retreat into their own positions and unleash barrages at everyone else. Sustainability is still different. Maybe because of its bendiness, it is difficult to find anyone who is violently against sustainability. It is a concept that offers the opportunity for dialogue. Its exact meaning will evolve over time. Its malleability today allows different people and different groups to explore what meanings it might have that could move us collectively forward. Think of sustainability not as a word but rather as a forum for conversation – it may include everything from the politics of transition to a Blairite 'sustainable growth', which meant precsiely the opposite (it meant carrying on growing) but it does at least mean there has to be a conversation about meanings and directions.

Like democracy, freedom, love, loyalty, truth, justice – sustainability is what Gallie called an essentially contested concept that has what Professor John Robinson of the University of British Columbia calls 'constructive ambiguity'. Its strength lies not in constraining its meaning but in what is probably an endless journey of exploration towards many meanings.

Of course, we don't want everything to be sustainable. Nobody argues for sustainable inequality, sustainable poverty, sustainable terrorism or a myriad other things. Yet we talk about sustainable business, sustainable finance, sustainable development, even sustainable consumption, a term that some consider an oxymoron. None of us yet knows what any of this means. But we seem to be able to create a remarkable unity in believing that we should explore these ideas. Nobody has the answer – and we should resist the siren calls of those who pretend that they do. Or those who try to equate sustainability with a narrow green agenda. Yet we do have a positive milieu for a broad discussion around all of these areas. We should use the opportunity.

It is true that some people criticise the malleability of 'sustainability' because it provides cover for those who want to subvert the environmental agenda. Poli, in a chapter entitled *From Compromise to Fraud* says that: "conservative groups and the traditional (over-polluting) industries allied with the emerging countries and used the Sustainable Development compromise to slow down and stop a substantial ecological reconversion of the industrial production."[65] We understand perfectly that ambiguity can be, and will be, exploited. But we believe, over time, that more confluence and practical progress will be made by using frameworks that encourage broad participation rather than those that create warring ideological cults, each convinced of the moral superiority of their own particular position.

A case in point is the long-running, largely pointless and shamefully wasteful COP process that has, for twenty years, fruitlessly and at great cost, created an adversarial atmosphere that made reaching any form of agreement largely impossible. The idea that some 200 countries would sign up to a uniform, legally binding agreement with externally verifiable metrics while accepting differentiated responsibility was always a nonsense that belonged in a looking-glass world. It took twenty years of wasted time and resources with ever increasing carbon emissions before things came to their senses in Paris in 2015. The French steered through a consensus that finally abandoned the fiction of broad, legally binding agreements and instead created a framework for the creation of coalitions of the willing to share know-how, technology and funding on a voluntary basis and as best suits their individual circumstances.

Some have condemned this approach as, at best imperfect, at worst a sell-out. In reality it is much more likely to create an atmosphere that encourages positive progress than the ideologues' counter-productive obsession with holding governments' feet to the fire in an attempt to force them into signing up to impractical and politically suicidal emission targets that most have no idea how to achieve.

## About subsidies

The call for subsidies for 'green' industries has for many years formed the centrepiece of environmental lobbying. While acknowledging that the subsidy habit will be difficult to eliminate totally, in principle we would discourage the use of direct-to-producer subsidies in any major way to incorporate environmental considerations into policy areas. There are many reasons for this.

Subsidies end up being distorting, have many unintended consequences and, especially when implemented early, can make matters worse. Agricultural subsidies, and especially the EU's Common Agricultural Policy, have resulted over decades in mountains of waste and a huge amount of environmental damage. Well-meaning subsidies directed at so called bio-fuels such as ethanol were initially pushed by the environmental lobby and gratefully accepted by farmers. They have not only disrupted food systems but have ended up with fuels that cost more in energy to produce than the energy that those fuels provide. The examples are endless. As Otto Scharmer and Katrin Kaufer put it in their book *Leading From The Emerging Future*: "Over time...[subsidies] become part of the problem rather than the solution."[66]

Direct-to-producer subsidies are socially unjust. They represent a massive transfer of wealth from the less well off (ordinary taxpayers) to the wealthy – the owners and shareholders of larger entities and corporations as well as other powerful vested interests that are capable of lobbying for and eventually receiving the subsidies. Germany's much vaunted *Energiewende* is one such example, where massive subsidies have enriched landowners and corporations at the expense of ordinary citizens. In the same spirit, we would, of course, argue for dramatic reductions in subsidies that continue to support the use of fossil fuels.

Subsidies generate and encourage rent-seeking behaviour. However much governments make clear that subsidies are intended to be temporary, their eventual withdrawal invariably generates howls of pain from vested interests, threats of job losses, and promises of all other manner of apocalyptic outcome. Funds used for subsidies are better directed to improving the plight of the poorest in society rather than enriching the wealthiest.

Subsidies cannot have an appreciable long term impact. Commenting as part of the inquiry into the development of a sustainable financial system led by the United Nations Environmental Programme (UNEP), Mark Carney, governor of the Bank of England, said that there is no fiscal solution to the sustainability challenge. In other words, the amounts of investment needed to transform a clearly unsustainable system to a more sustainable one can't be met by the limited funds available to governments. Meaningful change can only be achieved by attracting a proportion of the some $450 trillion of private capital available in global financial markets. The more we get into the habit of relying on subsidies (or philanthropy) to address environmental and social issues, the longer we risk delaying our search for ways to attract private finance in bulk. We risk creating a mirage of progress where none, in fact, exists because the approach – relying on subsidies – is itself unsustainable.

Finally, we should consider the human and social impact of subsidies. As some farmers in Southern Spain, recipients of significant EU subsidies, put it: "Yes, subsidies have helped us financially, but they have totally destroyed any sense of dignity we had in our work." Or, as the farmer in Somerset put it: "I could get subsidies but I never have and never will apply for them. Once they give you subsidies they want to control your whole life."

No Liberal could possibly be comfortable with any of this. Which is why Andalucian sheep farmer Santiaga calls subsidies *caramelos envenenados* – poisoned sweets.

Subsidies tend to undermine innovation. But an obsessive regulatory approach to subsidies, like that presided over by the European Union can also prevent local activity and entrepreneurial innovation too. These things matter and an enlightened pragmatism is required. Subsidies implemented by bodies such as the EU, like the CAP that encourages environmentally destructive behaviour, have major effects, spread like a malignant growth across the whole of Europe affecting millions of people – not to mention millions of hectares of land. Nobody can innovate, experiment or do things differently because that involves losing the subsidy. Once these mistakes become embedded, they become largely irriversible.

## The role of regulation

How many of us would happily fly with an airline that, if that were possible, decided to opt out of airline safety regulations? How many of us would put our money or investments with a totally unregulated bank of investment house?

Those on the right of the political spectrum have, since the Thatcher-Reagan era, decided to equate regulation with 'red tape'. They have mounted a war on regulation and turned de-regulation into a religion. Yet, regulation is not only a public good, it has the potential to make industry more competitive and more forward looking.

Taking the pharmaceutical industry as just one example, the US is both the largest market and has some of the best—and toughest—regulatory regimes. As a result, regulation by the Food and Drug Administration has become the global gold standard. US companies used to dealing with such regulation have become the global leaders in the industry to the extent that competitors in other countries have been more or less wiped out. The foreign companies that remain now structure their businesses to FDA standards. Similar examples abound in other industries.

We believe that well thought-out, forward-looking regulation forms an essential component of environmental policy. Regulators' primary duty is to the citizen and the consumer. Yet, modern regulation has the opportunity to extend that purpose without diluting it. By pre-empting the requirements of the future and being bold, clear, decisive, and not changing direction every five minutes, regulators can also help lift the standards, and thereby the competitiveness, of the industries that they regulate. In the environmental realm, the task should be to improve regulation so that it achieves both of these aims rather than sacrificing one for the other. Well designed environmental regulation will improve the health and well-being of citizens while making sure that industry is tooled up and ahead of the game compared to competitors in less regulated markets.

But to achieve that, regulators need to break the habit of backward-looking regulation – regulation that is designed as a reaction to past problems. This rarely works as it is usually outdated before it reaches the light of day. Instead, regulators should be designing forward-looking regulation that asks the questions: what sort of industry and what sort of behaviours do we want to be successful in the future? How can we design regulations that promote such industries?

Besides backward-looking regulatory habits, a further block to progress is resistance by those corporations that shun change, preferring instead lazily to stick with the status quo while managing to capture the regulators to do their bidding. As a result we see, for instance, a progressive dilution on what is allowed to be classified as an 'organic' product. In a recent case, 'organic' ladies knickers (yes, we're confused too) were withdrawn from the market because they were found to contain traces of a carcinogenic pesticide (we're even more confused). Following the Volkswagen emissions scandal, the European Commission, largely under pressure from a supposedly environmentally conscious Germany, decided to allow car manufacturers to exceed the prescribed emission limits by as much as half.

This behaviour amounts to a fraud on citizens perpetrated by regulators in conspiracy with a few corporations. A Liberal politics does not tolerate such behaviour and is prepared to use regulatory powers to drive forward-looking change.

Fortunately, many progressive businesspeople understand the

opportunity. That is why some years ago a coalition of companies lobbied the state government in California to increase the amount of environmental regulation knowing that this would force forward-looking change and make the economy more robust and more sustainably competitive. As we wrote in our 2015 pamphlet *A Radical Politics For Business* (see Chapter 5): "What has happened is that the major energy of business has shifted behind radical change.... business is emerging again – as it once was – as a radical force in the way the future is being shaped."[67] Well thought-out regulation has an immense role to play in helping business along that path.

We are not arguing here for single-focus environmental regulation that ignores reality. In an attempt to improve air quality, Schipol Airport in Amsterdam recently introduced rules designed to convert all taxis picking up from the airport to Tesla electric cars. One taxi driver explained the impact of these rules. He now has to purchase a car that costs nearly twice as much as it would otherwise cost. Battery life is insufficient for him to do a full day's work without having to sit for two hours for the batteries to re-charge. And the cars need major expense to replace batteries after only limited mileage compared to a diesel-powered car that ran almost for ever.

This is a clear example of poor regulation that pushes for environmental gain without looking at the bigger picture and in the absence of appropriate technology being available. It is this sort of unreasonable behaviour that, rightly, turns people against environmental regulation.

### Dumping our garbage

On recent trips to India and Japan, one couldn't help but notice the different attitudes that the two societies have to their lived environment. In Japan, you can eat off the streets. There is no litter and everything is scrupulously clean. When our hotel manager was showing us out to the bus stop, he stopped to pick off the middle of the street a tiny piece of paper that had been dropped – either inadvertently or, one supposes, by a tourist. In India, we visited a 'natural space' where families go to enjoy a little bit of countryside. The hill underneath the viewing platform was one large rubbish dump. Of course, the existence of such a rubbish dump simply encouraged everyone who visited to continue dumping their garbage on top of it.

In which of these environments would most of us prefer to live? Those who prefer the latter should read no further. But it's possible that they may be few and far between.

Today, in most of the Western world, dumping our garbage in the street, into our neighbours' garden or in areas of outstanding natural beauty is considered unacceptable and such habits horrify most of us. Yet we continue to allow our industrial society first of all to generate a huge amount of garbage and then freely to dump its detritus into the environment in which we all live. Our failure to tackle externalities – the ability of some to dump their costs on others – is arguably the biggest environmental issue that has always faced us. It is also an issue that goes to the heart of what we understand by wealth creation. Is our industrial society really creating wealth or is it simply stealing it from one place and putting it in another?

As Umair Haque puts it in *The New Capitalist Manifesto*: "Shareholder value isn't a reliable measure of whether authentic economic value has been created. It is value that can be transferred from other stakeholders rather than created anew."[68]

In other words, we live in an extractive economy where value is extracted from one place and simply transferred to another with minimal value added in the process – and in many cases value is actually destroyed. So, to reiterate the point that environmental issues do not stand alone, the questions related to externalities are not 'merely environmental', they go to the very heart of the sustainability of our economies and our ability to continue to create prosperity and well-being. A Liberal politics fit for the twenty-first century recognises, frames and addresses these issues for what they are. They are not 'green' issues: they are questions related to some of the fundamental structures of our economies that need re-thinking.

This, not narrow electoral considerations, is why environmental issues are natural Liberal territory. Because the very origin of Liberal thought and political Liberalism is about challenging deeply embedded social and economic structures and imagining the world anew. That is what our rapidly deteriorating environment challenges us to do once more today.

## Transforming industrial practice

There is no doubt that, over the decades, we have made progress in many aspects of industrial practice. CFCs have been banned. The standards imposed on the disposal of industrial waste have risen dramatically and, in many countries, continue to rise. And very many other examples. Yet these efforts, valuable as they have been, have largely been approached as attempts to solve individual issues, to ban individual pollutants one by one. Only relatively recently have we started to understand that we need to consider, and make inroads into, system level change.

We have understood that the economic system of the industrial age needs to be replaced by one that focuses in parallel on creating social, environmental and economic (not just financial) benefits. Hence the rise of triple bottom line accounting.

Some are now going beyond that. We outlined in Chapter 3 how the culture of the modern has had a soul-destroying effect. Recognising this, Commonland Foundation, a new Dutch organization focused on restoring landscapes, has added a fourth requirement to the triple bottom line – they require their projects also to provide a return of *inspiration*. In other words they want their work also to feed the human soul.[69]

In time, all this will doubtless lead to the instututional reform without which change cannot scale up. But, so far, most innovation is coming from within the business world itself. Some of it is driven by visionary leaders who are determined to create a different business model. Other initiatives are driven by corporate self-interest – a realisation that continuing to pursue the outdated industrial model is bad for business. What is the role of Liberal politics in all of this? We suggest that the first role is to look at, and learn from, what is happening out there among the leaders in this field. We will therefore start by looking at a couple of pioneer examples.

Patagonia, a US outdoor clothing company founded by environmentally conscious outdoor adventurer Yvon Chouinard, has initiatives designed not only to reduce the amount it pollutes and increase the amount it recycles, but also to reduce the amount of its clothing that consumers buy. This puts the company well ahead of other companies in environmentally responsible behaviour. In spite of being at the cutting edge, Patagonia's website frankly admits: "We are in the earliest stages of learning how what we do for a living both threatens nature and fails to meet our deepest human needs. The impoverishment of our world and the devaluing of the priceless undermine our physical and economic well-being."[70]

As a result of this thinking, Patagonia focuses on the triple bottom line and works to improve social, environmental as well as economic value. It publishes annually the impact that its activities have on the environment and works to reduce that impact year by year.

Other corporations, foreseeing the impact of resource depletion on their business are working to make sure that they replenish their vital resources more rapidly than they deplete them. Heineken and PepsiCo both understand that their business will cease to exist if water becomes even scarcer than it already is. Both have embarked on water conservation and restoration measures. In India, PepsiCo claims that it now produces more water than it uses in its products. These companies are changing the industrial model that used to consider natural resources just like another disposable item – something to be mined to extinction before moving on – to something they themselves have to produce in order to sustain their business.

In a similar vein, a number of corporations are re-shaping their business to be part of a circular economy rather than a linear economy. They design and manufacture their products and their whole supply chain, not only to use recycled products but in such a way that, after use, these products can themselves then be collected and re-cycled – and again, and again, and again. Some companies, such as carpet maker Interface, will also re-cycle other companies' products, so that they are not just waste neutral but waste positive.

While these innovations are often driven by forward looking

leadership or by corporate self-interest, they also reflect a significant change in social attitudes. Surveys have shown that the millennial generation put social responsibility much higher than previous generations when they evaluate companies they seek out for employment – and are much more willing to change jobs if they feel that their employing organisation does not have a sense of purpose. One lady who works in a senior position for a major international bank put it like this: "They pay me a lot of money, but I can't find the motivation to come in to work here any more. What we do has absolutely no purpose other than making a few people rich."

Her superiors wanted to retain her because she was a star performer. But all they had to offer was more money. Needless to say, that didn't work. Apart from driving change in large organizations, this cultural shift has also spawned large numbers of social entrepreneurs – another source of innovative business practice.

Because all this innovation is happening in the marketplace, is it not reasonable to take the *laissez faire* approach of the political right and let the market solve it all? No. There is a role for government – and it's a very big one. A Liberal politics would do what it has always done – encourage further experimentation, seek out what is at the cutting edge of progress and use political power, not to protect the laggards and the wealthy incumbents (the politics of the right), nor to take direct control and pretend it can run everything from the centre (the politics of the left) but to leverage existing successful, forward looking initiatives into large scale transformational change.

In regulatory terms, the attitude should be that, if all these cutting edge companies are doing all of this and being profitable and highly successful, so can everyone else. These leaders provide the model on which a future-oriented economy can be built. Governments should look for the outliers who are leading the way and use their experience and expertise to design regulation that pushes other corporations to reach the same, perfectly achievable high standards. The challenge is to resist the not inconsiderable pressure from the laggards – who will always form the bulk of industrial activity – to maintain the status quo.

This Liberal approach to regulation must be tough and uncompromising. It is the way to transform the meaning of competitiveness into a race to the top rather than the right wing, de-regulatory approach to competitiveness which turns economies into a race to the bottom. Or the left's approach which is not to consider competitiveness very much at all.

In specific terms, there is nothing to stop triple bottom line reporting from becoming the norm – imposed by regulation if necessary – and with a requirement to reduce impact year on year. The standard responses by the laggards to such suggestions are twofold:

- They will destroy industries and kill jobs.
- It can only be done after we have developed globally agreed common standards of measurement.

The first objection clearly does not have to be true, as many corporations are now showing. It is only true for lazy or incompetent management. The second objection is a tired delaying tactic. The triple bottom line concept is well established and methodologies exist to measure performance across all these parameters. True, the methodologies are not perfect. But what is?

The whole industrial and financial system measures itself by internationally agreed accounting standards. Yet, in the wake of scandals, bankruptcies and financial meltdowns, who would argue that our painstakingly developed international accounting standards are perfect? The search for perfection is just a smokescreen for stopping progress, and progress is what we need.

Regulation is one tool that can be used to address the issue that most 'wealth' is currently being created at the expense of others – what Umair Haque calls 'thin value' and economist Jack Hirshleifer calls 'socially useless' value. Incentives to encourage better industrial practices are another.

Benefit Corporations or B-Corps are US designed entities that "meet the highest standards of verified social and environmental performance, public transparency, and legal accountability, and aspire to use the power of markets to solve social and environmental problems." They are a growing phenomenon and have well developed and documented standards of behaviour, measurement and audit that go to the triple bottom line concept. They are starting to spread to Europe. But they are not yet a recognised corporate form in company law except in Italy which established the *Societá Benefit* on the US model. Enshrining B-Corporations in company law would allow both private and public corporations to choose to operate under that form.

In the evolving cultural and economic environment, companies that are focused on creating wealth while adding social and environmental value may be much more likely to attract investor interest than those whose success depends on extracting social and environmental value, and have no idea how to cope when the music eventually stops. Since B-Corporations are also measurably and verifiably adding social and environmental value, they should also perhaps be subject to lower rates of corporate tax, since they are already making contributions that reduce the public expenditure that would otherwise be required for corrective action.

Finally, there is another tool easily available to governments to encourage a sustainable economy – public procurement policies. Were governments to set high social and environmental standards for all companies eligible to bid for public procurement contracts, standards of industrial practice would rapidly rise.

As we can see, it does not take much imagination to envision a world of transformed industrial practice. Many in business itself are already showing the way. Neither is it impossible to come up with practical approaches where policy initatives can accelerate positive change. Yet inertia persists because the political power of the incumbent laggards remains greater than that of the innovators. They exercise that power through strength in numbers, political lobbying and financial contributions to those political parties that defend the status quo. All that Liberalism was born to tear down.

But a further block comes from the institutional inertia and the inherent conservativism of established institutions. We will not attempt here to go through all the institutional reforms that will be necessary to allow a more positive future to emerge except to say that this, too, should be natural Liberal territory. But we will address one particular sector that, as we have shown in previous chapters, plays a vital role in either enabling or stifling change – the financial sector.

## Sustainable finance
As we outlined in previous chapters, the financial services industry is not performing its core functions because so many companies

have shifted their core purpose from smoothing the flow of capital across the whole economy with minimum frictional cost, to using market power to increase transactional costs so that they can maximise their own and their shareholders' wealth.

In the context of this chapter, an even deeper issue arises. The financial services industry has developed to serve the extractive industrial age. It has therefore developed tools that both enable and encourage the core issue we have outlined earlier – the transfer of wealth rather than its creation.

We mentioned earlier the UNEP Inquiry into how we can move towards a financial system that supports a sustainable economy.[71] We will not reproduce here the conclusions and recommendations of that work as readers can examine the detail for themselves. Instead, we draw out some of the main conclusions and examine the implications for a Liberal politics.

The first lesson is that there is no magic bullet. Nobody knows what the answer should, or could, be and it is unlikely that someone (or some group of people, however clever) could sit down, design the perfect financial system and then implement it. The way forward was to encourage experimentation – stimulate and liberate individuals and groups to try out different approaches and see what works. This approach is perfect Liberal politics and is perfectly in line with how twenty-first century companies and economies are developing.

We live in a complex, organic non-linear system. The nineteenth and twentieth century ideas of deliberate, rational design followed by linear implementation no longer works. In an organic, fast-moving business and financial environment, progress happens by opening up to experimentation from which successes will emerge, and where some degree of failure is not only tolerated but celebrated as a learning exercise. In other words, it is an entrepreneurial rather than a bureaucratic approach. It is human, not technocratic.

The second lesson to emerge is that much of the creative and innovative policy approaches are happening in developing countries. There are two possible reasons for this. The first is that developed countries, bruised by the financial crash, have become cautious and enveloped in backward-looking regulation that has stifled innovation. The second is that emerging economies understand better the impact of environmental degradation on their future prospects. Brazil's economy, for instance, is highly dependent on its natural capital. To protect this asset, the BOVESPA Stock Exchange developed, in 2005, a corporate sustainability index. Since 2008, the Central Bank of Brazil has introduced measures to strengthen the management of socio-environmental risk and a judgment by the Superior Court of Justice suggested that financial institutions could face potentially unlimited liability for environmental damage caused by borrowers.

Also, in 2011, the banking regulator required banks to monitor environmental risks as part of the implementation of Basel III's Capital Adequacy requirements and, in 2014, required all banks to establish socio-environmental risk systems. India has Priority Sector Lending requirements for banks to allocate 40 per cent of all lending to sectors that are considered core eonomic development priorities to which renewable energy has now been added. China has made environmental disclosure a mandatory requirement of its securities legislation, has launched a massive green bonds programme, has extended mandatory environmental liability insurance and has established a firm legal framework for environmental lender liability.

Some innovation is also happening in developed economies. These range from requirements in corporate sustainability reporting in France. Or the UK Green Investment Bank and the requirement that pension funds disclose whether they take environmental, social and ethical factors into account in their investment process. Or the many state level initiatives in the USA, ranging from insurance regulation requiring the inclusion of climate change risks, to initiatives to expand the impact investing market.

All these changes can be summarised as policies that push the financial system to achieve three things:

- Extend its investment horizon and discourage practices that focus exclusively on short term financial returns.
- Increase transparency and accountability for the environmental and social damage caused by investment decisions, and
- Focus the public balance sheet onto a sustainable economy and encourage private finance to follow public investment priorities.

Once again, changing the financial system to support a sustainable rather than an extractive economy is neither unimaginable nor unachievable. But it takes concerted effort at government level if it is to be achieved.

## Keeping the lights on – but less of them

Without energy, our whole way of life would collapse. The paradox is that our current pattern of energy generation and consumption is also threatening our way of life. It is therefore no surprise that energy is rapidly emerging as one of the key policy areas for the twenty-first century. And there are no easy or perfect solutions here either.

What do we require from our energy system? What we would all like is to have a clean, affordable, safe, reliable and secure supply of energy. Most people would agree with that statement. Yet each adjective used in that sentence is relative rather than absolute. There is no such thing as perfectly clean energy – just cleaner than what we have today. There is no perfectly safe and secure source of energy supply. And so on. Unfortunately, the energy debate has, over the last few decades, been reduced to an unseemly and unproductive battle between fossil fuels and renewable energy sources. While there is general agreement that shifting our economies away from reliance on fossil fuels is desirable for many reasons, actually achieving such a shift in any reasonable time frame has proved challenging.

Pragmatically, it is likely that some elements of a fossil fuel economy will remain the reality for many decades to come. These are difficult issues and we, the authors,find ourselves on different sides of the argument about shale gas extraction and nuclear energy, though clearly some kind of transition period is inevitable.

Where we do agree is that the widespread use of nuclear energy is likely be limited if for no other reason than cost. The European pressurised reactors, for instance, are so costly and complex that some have argued they might not actually be constructable. Smaller, modular reactors may be much more viable and even newer technologies will emerge. That isn't yet clear.

What about renewable sources? Those interested in environmental and social considerations should abandon the myth that our current renewable sources somehow represent the ideal energy source. We all know their significant faults. They are unreliable as continual sources of energy. If we were to replace all our energy supply with renewable sources, the land mass that would be required would destroy vast swathes of land and destroy biodiversity. Wind farms kill a large number of birds which is why, until recently, NGOs like the Royal Society for the Protection of Birds was, at best, lukewarm about them as an energy source. Solar panels depend for their production on mined rare earths, many of which come from China, thereby raising significant geoplitical questions about energy security.

None of this is intended to minimise the importance of developing renewable sources of energy. It is simply to point out that that doing so does not represent the panacea that some seem to make it out to be – at least for the moment. The energy question is somewhat more complex than simply the replacement of fossil fuels with renewable energy sources.

Much has been written about energy policy and it is not our intention to reproduce it here. Rather we focus on three main themes of how a Liberal politics would translate into energy policy: creating a low energy economy, decentralisation of responsibility and investment in energy R&D.

*The low energy economy*

As indicated above, much of the debate about energy has been focused on the supply side. Discussions about energy efficiency have seemed to be somewhat of an add-on and restricted to making incremental efficiency improvements. We suggest that much progress towards reaching many of the stated objectives of energy policy could be made if we placed as a central question – how can we create a low energy *economy*?

Economic development has always seemed to be linked to increasing energy use. But in recent years the link between economic growth (as measured by GDP) and energy use (the energy intensity) has been broken and less energy is being used per unit of GDP. This is particularly the case in developed economies, because of a combination of energy efficiency and a shift from manufacturing-based economies to service-based economies. Even so, the policy focus so far has been mainly on efficiency. This has produced some results and can go much further. But, on its own, it will provide diminishing returns, because efficiency is all about doing what we've always done but doing it better.

To go further, we need to re-think our economies as a whole and imagine what a truly low energy economy could look like and what we could do to get there. To some extent, in a low energy economy, questions about the sources of energy generation become secondary since total energy consumption, and therefore the environmental, security and cost issues associated with different energy sources, would be considerably lower.

Technologies for, for example, building eco-homes homes are well developed and could provide signifcant lifetime savings in both materials and energy use. But building eco-homes probably remains the exception rather than the rule. Changing building regulations could very easily provide a huge boost to building them with consequent lower energy costs for families.

Similarly, we have to question the wisdom of the huge subsidies that flow daily to high energy intensity industries. If the objective were the creation of a low energy economy, such subsidies would disappear. True, this might cause some of these industries to relocate elsewhere. But why is this a problem? They can be replaced by new, clean, low energy industries that would drive a low energy economy and make countries more competitive in the long run.

Finally, we are unlikely to get significant change until we modify the incentive structure. The current incentive structure that links the revenue and profits of energy companies to the amount of energy that is consumed does nothing to drive towards a low energy economy. A new incentive structure needs to be developed that rewards energy companies more the less energy they sell, while making sure that this does not result in removing the financial incentives from consumers and industry to be more energy efficient. This involves a findamental change in how we think about the economics of energy supply and demand. Creating such an incentive structure will be challenging but not impossible. For instance, New York State's 2014 energy plan understands the importance of changing the energy incentive systems and looks to "enable and facilitate new energy business models for utilities, energy service companies and customers to be compensated for activities that contribute to grid efficiency."[72]

We also believe that we should be aiming for a low energy economy not merely a low carbon economy. In the wake of the Volkswagen scandal, it has become clear that merely being low carbon does not mean clean. Modern diesel engines may lower carbon emissions but they instead spew out polluting particulate matter that is damaging to human health. Similarly, Germany's *Energiewende* has, preversely, resulted in an increase in carbon and other emissions emissions as the only commercially viable backup energy provided for the push to renewables has turned out to come from coal-fired energy plants. Some claim that this increase in pollution will be temporary and it will all come right in the end.

A single-minded and narrow focus on carbon emissions will help future issues arising from climate change. But if the focus is exclusively on carbon, this may be achieved at the cost of higher alternative pollutants reaching the atmosphere. A low energy economy is, on other hand, one that has the potential to reduce all pollutants, reduce energy costs for all, increase energy security and make economies more competitive in the long run.

*Decentralising energy responsibility*
Our energy systems are still largely based on centralised generation systems with complex and expensive distribution networks. Not only is this an outdated way of thinking, it puts businesses and consumers at the mercy of centralised energy supply systems and reduces energy security. With the development of both renewable and other technologies that work on smaller scales, such a complex and expensive system can be made less important.

Centralised power plants were initially established to achieve economies of scale. But, such economies have largely run out. Also, a major part of the cost of power supply now lies not with its generation but with its supply, through complex grid systems. These systems are inefficient in terms of the amount of energy lost through distribution and they also mean less energy security, as most energy supply failures now originate in the grid. Distributed generation therefore brings both efficiency and security gains while having the potential to devolve responsibility, at least in part, to local government and local communities – giving them both more control and more accountability for their local energy needs.

Moving toward such devolved systems is fully aligned with the Liberal philosophy of devolving power and responsibility to the lowest possible levels and encouraging communities to be self-sufficient. It also implies devolving responsibility further, to make individual estates, institutions and homes, as self-sufficient in energy as possible. That sense of independence is a Liberal emotion, and it explains some of the emerging divisions in the Tea Party movement in the USA, for example, and similar divisions in Spain and Australia where the old providers are trying to prevent people from generating their own solar energy. It is absolutely clear where Liberals stand on this division – for responsibility and energy independence.

Technologies exist to start moving seriously towards a distributed system like that. They include, among others, combined heat power (CHP) and micro-CHP, fuel cells, micro-turbines, roof top solar panels, reciprocating engines, and others.

One policy approach is to combine communities into a single energy unit making them combined supplier and customer. Communities would then benefit from increased buying power while being able to make their own infrastructure and planning decisions for local energy supply. Communities could then decide for themselves whether, for instance, to install local micro turbines for their own energy supply or to keep buying more energy from the grid. This could dramatically change the equation when communities are faced with decisions as to whether to allow wind turbines to be built in their area – something that is currently heavily opposed by many communities who see the disadvantages but gain little advantage as the energy so generated feeds into central grids rather than their own community supply.

In the same way, local authorities would have an incentive to encourage or require the installation of solar panels or other energy sources for all new house builds in their areas as well as retro-fitting existing builds.

Finally, in the drive towards a low energy economy, local communities would be able to use both local market mechanisms as well as local regulation or peer pressure to reduce energy usage patterns – something that has worked well in some areas that have tried it – like some towns and cities in Oregon.

Whichever policy approach proves to be the most practicable given local circumstances, we suggest that decentralisation of part of the responsibility for how to deal with energy supply and demand to local communities will unleash a wave of experimentation as different communities try different approaches. Out of such experiments will emerge some successful models that can then be reproduced in other places. None of this is possible while all decisions are made centrally through a monolithic structure peopled by individuals who think they know what's best for every community in the land.

## Energy R&D

We have argued that energy will likely be one of the most crucial policy areas in the twenty-first century. We are also all painfully aware that current technologies leave much to be desired. We therefore suggest that significant investment in energy related Research and Development should occupy a prominent place in energy policy.

In the Copenhagen Consensus on Climate project, 28 climate economists and a panel of experts including three Nobel laureates concluded that, with every dollar spent on clean energy R&D, you can avoid a hundred times more climate change than money spent on installing current renewables. While we believe that the two should not be mutually exclusive options – and that climate change is not the only issue that should drive energy policy – the study does give some indication of the importance, and possible returns, of increased investment in energy R&D.

## Re-vitalising rural economies

Imagine taking a large, scattered but poor rural community and re-vitalising it. Increasing not only its economic potential but also its attractiveness for the young to remain there, rather than fleeing towards the city - to make it appealing both for new people to come to live there and for the creation of an mixed economy based on agriculture, tourism and some light industry. And all done in a way that helps restore the environment locally and globally.

This is one of the projects that Commonland Foundation is embarked upon in Southern Spain. The area covers 630,000 hectares. Encouraged by the experience of a few pioneering farmers, two thousand of them across the region are being mobilised to change their farming habits. They are converting to regenerative agricultural practices; shifting from the monoculture routine to a mixed crop economy, restoring natural spaces to supply sustainable ecosystem services to the farming community, while providing wildlife habitat. They are bringing in processing and marketing skills and infrastructure so that added value can be captured at the site of production, and developing the local sites of historical interest to offer combined historical and eco-tourism attractions to potential visitors. And all done so that the multiple projects are investible by private investors rather than depending forever on government handouts or philanthropy.

It is all at a very early stage. But the local population is energised and there is an immense sense of the possible. It's a twenty year project – well beyond the interest horizons of most political parties – or most investors for that matter. Yet the local community can already envision a world that is different from that which they inhabit today – scraping a living from ever more degraded soils, producing a single crop that puts them at the mercy of commodity markets, seeing most of the value of their work captured by the global supply chain, and being forever dependent on subsidies.

Why have we given up on rural communities? Why have we come to believe that the only way they can survive is through a massive programme of subsidy? Why do we simply accept the mass movement of people to the city? And why do we not only tolerate but, through ill-conceived and out-dated subsidy programmes, continue to encourage agricultural practices that are not only unprofitable but destructive of our environment? It is all highly illiberal yet we seem unable to imagine any alternative.

The current system of EU subsidies under the Common Agricultural Policy is one of the main barriers to progress in the Spanish project we describe above. Almost every practice that improves the environment makes farming more sustainable, and tries to capture more added value locally, leads to loss of EU subsidies. The other main block is the force of habit. Apart from the subsidy issue, the most common objection to changing farming habits comes in the form of "but this is how we've always done it." But there is another way.

Farming occupies huge swathes of land. It uses vast amounts of water and the agricultural habits of the past centuries have destroyed our soils, making agriculture dependent on using chemical fertilizer that pollutes rivers and water supplies. Agricultural habits have also destroyed the natural resilience of the land now leading to ever increasing flood and drought cycles. And our rural environment no longer provides a viable habitat for the wildlife and the pollinators on which we all, including the farmers themselves, depend. All this in pursuit of an elusive efficiency designed to compete on a global scale. It has been one massive failure – for our environment, for our economies and for rural communities. Rural regeneration and its environmental context is, clearly, a vast subject. In this section we have chosen to address only three areas that we believe to be crucial: soil, resilience and the limits of globalisation.

*Restoring our soils*

As with industry, so with agriculture. Encouraged by misguided subsidy programmes, today's agricultural practices are extractive processes that, rather than preserving our soils, mine them until they are no longer productive. Thirty million acres of food producing soils are turned into desert every year. Twenty-four billion tonnes of degraded soil are then washed or blown away annually.

John Steinbeck's *The Grapes of Wrath* describes the mass migration of 1930s rural workers who had become impoverished by the conversion of their fields to Dust Bowl. Since then, the only thing that has changed is the emergence of ever more effective, and ever more polluting, chemical fertilizers. The organic food movement has tried partially to reverse this trend. But, as we have mentioned earlier, constant lobbying has stripped 'organic' of much of its meaning and of its potential to have any widespread positive impact.

What is needed is a wholesale shift to regenerative and holistic agricultural practices. Progressively adding organic matter to soils regenerates their nutritive potential, increases water absorption capacity (thereby reducing not only the amount of irrigation needed, but also decreasing flood potential). This can, over time, increase yields, reduce costs, and help with climate change. Combining regenerative agriculture with mixed crops, wildlife corridors, and restoring natural spaces next door, will make rural economies once more sustainable.

Neither are these changes only possible in arable farming. Soil restoration and moving towards mixed farming that includes natural spaces and livestock rotation in combination with arable land would all improve the productivity of our rural eeconomies and our environment. Livestock, rotated and well managed, can have positive rather than destructive effects on the land and, as some have suggested, can make livestock farming a practice that improves our ability to mitigate climate change rather than, as is now the case, being a major contributor towards it.

Yet this goes directly against the philosophy of so-called 'modern' intensive farming – practices that focus on monoculture, the separation of natural spaces from agricultural land, and the hard division between arable and livestock farming. Today's practices are part of the extractive economy that puts short term efficiency gains ahead of the development of sustainable rural economies. And, encouraged by subsidy, has destroyed most of our rural economies, and which renders many of them no longer viable. None of this is to argue against the use of modern technology. But technology can be used as a way of destroying the land and then trying to overcome the effects of that destruction – as has happened until now. Or it can be directed towards enhancing sustainable agricultural practices.

Alongside these methods of land restoration, we are seeing the emergence of agriculture as manufacturing. Growing some crops that previously occupied significant portions of land is now done in what can only be described as crop factories. Compact, intensive, with computer controlled lighting, airing and irrigation systems these factories can grow plants without the need to occupy huge swathes of land and without leaving the farmers at the mercy of the unpredictable weather. These new systems will not replace traditional agriculture but they usefully sit alongside it to produce economically viable crops with less land and environmental degradation than would otherwise be the case.

*Resilience*

Unsustainable, extractive agricultural practices do not just affect the farming community, they affect us all. Both water usage and flood risk have been significantly increased by today's agricultural practices. Which is why Living Lands, an international NGO, is working in South Africa to bring about change. Farmers were previously subsidised to run as many sheep as possible and to cut water channels into the land to help with run-off. Forests were wiped out, land was degraded and the result was a combination of lack of water supply to nearby towns and cities with uncontrollable floods during periods of heavy rain.

Local communities have started to reverse this trend. They have planted 3.7 million trees, are stopping land degradation and restoring water catchment systems. The result is less flooding, better land management and the sustainable provision of water to nearby Port Elizabeth – South Africa's fifth largest city. But perhaps the most remarkable aspect of this work is that much of it is funded by Santam, South Africa's largest agricultural insurer.

Santam understands the risks posed to their business by unsustainable agricultural practices and calculate that ever-increasing insurance premiums is not a viable solution. They have therefore invested in reducing their risk exposure because it is essential to the survival of their insurance business.

Once again, this response is diametrically opposed to the more common, finger in the dike, policy approaches where flood risk is met by yet more flood defences and yet more short-term technological fixes that do nothing to address the underlying causes. As always, it seems that some enlightened businesses are well ahead of a political class that seems more interested in high profile announcements of short-term fixes than in tackling root causes to the benefit of everyone.

A Liberal politics ought to, instead, address the root causes, sweep away all the barriers to improved agricultural practices and create rural economies that are once again inhabited, thriving and able to stand on their own two feet.

One final lesson from the South African experience. Today, there is excitement around the city as a political unit. That is all to be encouraged. But cities don't stand alone. They are surrounded by rural areas and the two interact at various levels. As we have seen above, rural agricultural practices affect the water supply of cities. The cities' detritus on the other hand affects surrounding rural areas. Cities should therefore not be treated as stand-alone units, either politically or economically. That would risk encouraging further growth of cities at the expense of surrounding rural communities.

Rather the appropriate unit is the city with its surrounding countryside. Treated as one unit, it is more likely that their interdependence will be more obvious and better managed so that both will prosper. We therefore question the recent move towards more elected city mayors, except when they cover city regions. While a welcome move towards more devolution, we believe that the political unit chosen is too limited.

## The limits of globalisation

The most common response to any attempts to revitalise rural economies is that it would make them 'uncompetitive' in a globalised world. As we have mentioned before, this position rests on the belief that globalisation is about a race to the bottom rather than a race to the top and that only extractive, short-term, efficient industrial practices can possible compete.

The reality is that there is an increasing demand from consumers for food products that are 'healthy' and originate from known and trustworthy sources. The new slow food and farm-to-table movements, and the seemingly inexorable rise of local farmers' markets, point to an increasing demand for real, fresh produce in preference to the tasteless, chemical infested, environmentally destructive food that emerges from the global supply chain. Current ideas of global competitiveness rest on the assumption that there is only one global commodity market for agricultural products. As is now abundantly clear, that is not the case and the importance of local markets and more sophisticated food consumers are increasing. That is not about regulation or about protectionism: quite the reverse, it is about challenge, competition and choice.

We are pressing against the limits of globalisation (see Chapter 4), where the downsides are starting to outweigh the benefits. The response is not a return to the tariff barriers of the past but rather, as we have described, it lies in policies that encourage thriving local economies alongside the benefits of globalisation. The approaches we have previously outlined, such as the use of local currencies, have great potential as levers to re-vitalise rural economies and transform them into communities that are more economically, socially and environmentally sustainable.

**

A Liberal politics does not address environmental issues in isolation. Neither does it focus on 'plant-a-tree' type policies that merely attempt to remediate environmental damage without addressing the root causes. Rather, it is a politics that uses environmental questions as another set of spectacles through which economies and communities can be viewed. Using these spectacles, we see an extractive, unsustainable industrial economy that creates little added value but merely transfers value from our common resources to a small proportion of the population. Luckily, emerging finance, energy and agricultural and industrial practices demonstrate that this is not the only way forward.

Pioneering efforts are underway in various parts of our economy to move towards a different economic model that is more sustainable and that can harvest our shared resources for the long term. A Liberal politics uses these pioneering approaches as the model and implements policies that, through regulation and incentive structures, makes them the norm.

# 7

# Turning public services inside out

*"So at last human society may become a friendly society—*
an Affiliated Order *of branches, some large and many small, each*
*with its own life in freedom, each linked to all ... So the* night's
insane dream of power over other men, without limit *and* without
mercy, shall fade. *So mankind in brotherhood shall bring back the*
*day."*
**William Beveridge, *Voluntary Action***


Sir William Beveridge was a friend of John Maynard Keynes and a
member of Keynes' informal group of former civil servants who
met every week from the start of the Second World War. They
called themselves the Old Dogs and they had cut their teeth in
Whitehall during the First World War, Keynes in economic policy
and Beveridge in social policy.

By the end of the war, both had inherited the world: Keynes'
economic design formed the basis for the assumptions that
underpinned the post-war world (in fact the American advisor
Harry Dexter White won the detailed battles over Bretton Woods,
though he would be unmasked later as a Soviet agent). Beveridge's
design for the welfare state formed the basis of post-war
reconstruction, not just in the UK but way beyond.

Both men were also Liberals, probably the central intellectual
figures in Liberalism of the twentieth century. Both also perhaps

the most misunderstood: just as Keynes' legacy was taken by the technocrats, a class of economist he had little time for, so Beveridge's legacy was taken over the by the centralisers, the God-like administrators of the post-war welfare state. Just as Keynes' legacy was being misused in the 1960s to pay for the Vietnam war, so Beveridge's legacy was misused to undermine the way in which working class communities supported each other – a process revealed in Young and Willmott's sociological classic *Family and Kinship in East London.*[73]

"The housewife of Britain has to accept that the *man in Whitehall really does know best,"* said Lord Shawcross in the 1940s.

"We are dealing with people who have no initiative or civic pride," said Newcastle's chief planning officer in 1963, revealing the contempt of the governing classes for the governed. "The task surely is to break up such groupings, even though people seem to be satisfied with their miserable environment and seem to enjoy an extrovert social life in their own locality."

Nobody would dare say things like that today, and the second quotation goes some way to explaining how working class neighbourhoods could have been so disastrously re-developed in the 1960s and 1970s. But the basic idea is deep in the DNA of British government at every level. British government does not believe it has much to learn from the local, whether it is local people or institutions. That is why the challenge from below is so important in public services, as everywhere else.

The role of the Liberal Party during this period has been to articulate the doubt that has given rise to the voluntary sector and so much else, about the viability of the technocratic approach. It has been a critique of industrial modernity, as we set out in

Chapter 2. But the real problem with Beveridge's legacy is that the basic assumptions were wrong. This is how his famous 1942 report set out the assumptions behind the finance of an NHS:

"No change is made in this figure as from 1945 to 1965, it being assumed that there will actually be some development of the service, and as a consequence of this development *a reduction in the number of cases requiring it.*"[74] [our italics]

This is where Beveridge discusses his assumptions about affordability, and here lies the problem. Because it assumes, as you can see here, that services would get cheaper over time, because need would be reduced. That was the assumption on which the new welfare state rested and it was wrong – in fact it has been wrong everywhere. Beveridge set out to slay what he called the Five Giants – Ignorance, Want, Squalor, Disease, Idleness. The problem is not that he failed to vanquish them. He killed them stone dead, but something he never expected happened. They came back to life again every generation and had to be slain all over again and, every time, it gets more expensive not less.

Through 60 years of peace and plenty, Beveridge's legacy has not managed significantly to narrow inequalities of income or health or to strengthen social solidarity. Neither, in general, has the welfare state successfully tackled the underlying reasons why problems emerge in the first place. Now it also has to cope with the implications of environmental degradation, an ageing society and a dysfunctional global financial system. Something has to change.

What went wrong? This is such an important question that we hardly dare ask it, in case it is taken as a political excuse to wind up the Beveridge experiment altogether, and because the failure of the welfare state to create a sustainable improvement in social welfare threatens to overwhelm the public finances.

It is true that Beveridge was in some ways a victim of his own success – the welfare settlement led to longer lives, which often (though not always) led to higher costs. It led to different diseases and to disabled children surviving into adulthood. These are partial explanations, but they don't really cover everything: why has health spending risen so fast for all generations, not just the old? Why is 80 per cent of NHS time spent dealing with chronic health problems? Why has crime risen so much in the same period? Why has social breakdown overwhelmed the caring services? It isn't just that people are living longer.

But Beveridge himself was more aware of this conundrum than his reputation suggests. He was aware that the Attlee government rolled out the NHS, for example, on lines very different to those he had suggested. He wrote an overlooked third report called *Voluntary Action*, which crystallised his thinking and his warnings about what might happen if the welfare state became too paternalistic, and if people's instincts for self-help, and their ability to find their own solutions, were allowed to atrophy.[75]

He wrote that the state had an important role, but equally important were what he called: "Room, opportunity and encouragement for voluntary action in seeking new ways of social advance... services of a kind which often money cannot buy".[76]

He was afraid that his reforms were encouraging people to focus passively on their needs. To emphasise his fears, he never used the term 'Welfare State', preferring the phrase 'Social Services State', which he used to highlight the individual's duties or services. By 1948, Beveridge doubted whether his 1942 report was enough to build the cohesive, fairer nation he was trying to achieve. This is not a simple argument. Membership of the self-help friendly societies peaked at around ten million in 1945, though there is some reason to suggest that voluntary action in general did not decline in the years that followed.[77] Yet there is no doubt that it *did* decline in those areas where the welfare state had become involved – healthcare, education, maybe also social care.

This narrative has become part of the critique of the Welfare State by the liberal wing of the Conservative Party. This is Phillip Blond: "The welfare state nationalised a previously mutual society and reformed it according to an individualised culture of universal entitlement."[78]

We need to take this seriously, especially as rationed public services increasingly use *need* as their currency of access. The only assets people have then are their own needs, which must be maximised if they are to access help. It is hardly surprising, in those circumstances, that needs seem to grow. But there is another problem as well, as the needs burgeon: the over-professionalization which Beveridge warned against seems to have widened the basic divide in all public services – between an exhausted, remote professional class and their clients, who are expected to remain passive and easy to process.

This is not just disempowering, but it can also be corrosive. It also brings what are a bundle of threats to the Beveridge legacy to a head – the maximisation of needs, the corrosion of voluntary action, and the social passivity. Added to which is the combination of inflation in public services and dwindling budgets, and (thanks to the Blair-Brown legacy) their dwindling effectiveness. Taken together, this looks like a Beveridge Crunch.

# The corrosion of effectiveness

We should look first at the ability of public services to deal effectively with people's needs, and here there are emerging problems. The targets regime was not introduced by Blair and Brown, but they turbocharged it, arguably driving up the performance of narrow measures like waiting times in Accident and Emergency departments with it. The trouble is that the targets fell foul of Goodhart's Law – that any measure used to control will always be inaccurate.

This was predictable. What was not predictable was the scale of the impact of Goodhart's Law on services when targets pretended to be able to provide transparency for every detail of what went on in the frontline. It shifted the purpose of services from delivering effective support to meeting target numbers, just as it diverted professionals from meeting needs to using clients as a means by which they could earn their targets. The experiment fatally shifted effort and resources in the wrong direction, spreading extra costs elsewhere in the system.[79]

The Blair and Brown years have been hailed as a period of investment in services. It was, of course, but this was investment fatally undermined by processes which undermined effectiveness, rendering services much more expensive – because targets were the ultimate centralising device. They hoovered up the available energy, imagination and flair of the organisation to make the figures look good.

There was at the same time a fly-on-the-wall documentary about airport security where the staff focused all their attention, not on spotting potential terrorists, but on spotting the fake terrorists sent to test their attentiveness by their managers – a slightly different skill. Imagine that same shift of resources across every public service and every service organisation. The waste and perversity that results will be absolutely vast.

The system thinker John Seddon produced the most coherent critique and probably the most practical alternative. In his latest book, *The Whitehall Effect*, he describes his first encounter with local government. Swale District Council called him in because the back office system the Department of Works and Pensions had told them to put in place for housing benefits seemed to be increasing the backlog – as we now know it does. Seddon set out the basic problem: imperial systems, like those built by public services during the Blair-Brown years – and especially inappropriate IT systems – can't absorb the kind of human variety they tend to get. This enormously boosts costs.[80]

The trouble is that some of these issues remain unresolved. Without some kind of numerical measures, how are politicians going to hold services to account? And if they don't use numerical targets, will these not just be imposed on them by the media? Seddon's answer is this: politicians should set the intentions of services and let managers find the best way to achieve them. This is what he says:

"Making leaders responsible for choices about measures and methods returns validity to inspection. Instead of inspecting for errors as laid down in checklists, inspectors will pose just one question: What are the methods and measures being used to achieve the purpose of the service?, and then check their validity."

This is exactly right but, in practice, this is only the beginning of a practical answer, because numerical systems of control are now so powerful and centralising, driven by IT. We still need to square the circle between the need for transparency and political responsibility and the need to use the frontline and human skills of service staff as they know best – and to allow from this very practical challenge from below.

## The corrosion of choice

One of the authors of this book had the experience of conducting an independent review for the coalition government into 'Barriers to Choice'.[81] Among the people who gave evidence was a woman with muscular dystrophy who had to see her consultant every six months, which meant a two-hour round trip plus half an hour or more in the waiting room. It meant going over a large river and paying a toll (which she would not have to pay if she was visiting a relative in prison), and all she says, when the doctor asks her how she is, is "I'm fine".

What she really wanted was to check in occasionally by phone, and see him when she was not fine. But she couldn't because his slots were full seeing people who were also fine. There is a clue here also about how to release capacity in the NHS, and other services: it might be to examine whether long-term patients might prefer to have a more flexible relationship with consultants.

This particular patient had tried and had been told by the consultant's secretary rather aggressively that, if she failed to turn up for her next appointment, she would be struck off the list. But what this story really reveals is a difference in understanding between patients and policy-makers about the meaning of the word 'choice'. It was a 'choice' about her treatment, in a sense, but not one that is recognised currently by the system in the UK.

When the idea of public service choice emerged in the US public school system, it was envisaged as a lever to force up quality. It allowed poor, excluded families to send their children to the best schools, when the inner city ghettos had tended to trap them in the worst ones. When school choice was introduced into the UK in 1994, it had a similar intention. It was intended as a means by which less privileged children could break into the middle class schools, and a means by which it might be possible to raise standards across the board. A similar idea lay behind NHS choice.

That was not quite how things have ended up. School choice has worked quite well in the UK – though less so perhaps in London, where exam results rose but choice is a mirage – mainly by lowering people's expectations. It is not so much choice as the right to express a preference.

Service choice is on the backburner in Whitehall these days, just as it is in other countries. This is partly because different ideologies – and different government departments – mean something completely different when they use the word, and these differences are not widely understood. For Liberals, choice means rights for consumers; for Conservatives it means privatisation. Under New Labour, choice was developed, rather expensively, by a group of economists as a way of raising standards. It has been politically controversial because of fears that choice would inevitably benefit those who are articulate and demanding enough to make use of it – though its intention was the opposite.

Ironically, it was developed by people who, paradoxically, were not very interested in choice. 'Choice' in Whitehall became shorthand for competition: the two terms are used interchangeably. The difficulty was that 'choice' and 'competition' are not actually the same, and the failure to distinguish them narrows the idea of choice in a way that makes it politically ambiguous. As service users know very well, there are times when choice and competition are aligned, but there are also times when they cancel each other out. This is so, for example, when the actual choice is made not by patients, but by service commissioners choosing between two alternative candidates for block contracts. Or when the weight of demand is such – as it is for some popular schools or GP surgeries – that the choice is made by the institution, not by the user. In both cases, there is competition, but no user choice.

This is a long-term problem for the choice agenda in the UK. It means that choice is politically unstable. It is controversial because it appears to have a hidden agenda (competition/privatisation) and an unspoken by-product (inequality). That makes it appear vulnerable to a change of political leadership, just as it is vulnerable to professionals who disapprove of, or misunderstand, it. In social care, the vast majority of professionals have bought into the agenda of control and personalisation, although there are disagreements about how this is best promoted. In other areas of public service, like parts of the NHS, 'choice' is sometimes seriously contested.

What really needs to happen is to broaden the idea of choice so that it breaks out of the confines of competition, and covers the kind of flexibility people want in the services they use. The new emphasis would be not so much on choosing between regulated options, but on making services flexible enough to suit individuals better – closer to the 'personalisation' agenda in social care, where service users can get budgets they can (theoretically, at least) use in ways they believe are best suited to their needs.

The most obvious difference between flexibility and competition is that it does not require a detailed regulatory infrastructure in quite the same way. We need to have general guidance about how flexibility can best be achieved, but not the kind of competition regulators (like Monitor, the sector regulator for health services in England) that are so controversial in the UK system.

The experience with personal budgets in social care suggests that risk-averse local administrators can frustrate the broad aims at local level. It also suggests that central regulations are not enough to guarantee personalisation locally. It suggests instead that the best approach would be to find ways to strengthen the confidence of service users to ask for something different, and perhaps provide duties on service providers to consider this.

This would be like a 'right to request' flexible service delivery. In each case, the provider would not be obliged to provide flexibility if it were impossible, but they would be obliged to explain why and that letter would have to be posted on their website. It would be aimed particularly at situations where systems or bureaucratic arrangements get in the way of what people need. For example, if they want the choice of a consultant who won't mind them asking lots of questions. Or to study Spanish at A-level when all that prevents them is their school's timetabling system. Or to go to bed later than 5pm when their carer comes round. These are basic flexibilities in the system which articulate people can often get now by being assertive, but which others can't. It provides that all-important challenge from below.

There are certainly possible objections to this kind of approach. Patients may choose badly. They may fail to take responsibility for the wider system, by misusing the flexibilities they are offered. There may also be higher costs from treating people more individually, and the costs will come before the potential savings are available. Financial innovations which tie professionals too closely to narrow numerical outcomes, like the current experiments with 'Payment By Results' may also make flexibility more difficult to achieve.

The cost issue is important. The evidence that flexibility can cut costs is ambiguous. Personal budgets in social care is an example of flexibility in action and, although there is considerable evidence of improved satisfaction – even improved outcomes (a recent Lancaster University study found that there was evidence of better well-being (63%) and better physical health (59%) – there is little evidence in the UK so far that it can cut costs.[82] But the evidence from Local Area Co-ordinators in Western Australia suggest that a more informal approach to disability and social care, which has flexibility at its heart, can cut costs by up to a third – and improve satisfaction with the service.[83]

The truth is that the costs of inflexibility – the failure to be effective – are absolutely enormous. One anecdote makes the point. It is about the doctor's surgery with the hedge outside which is trimmed once a year in the summer, and – when it is trimmed – a pile of rejected prescriptions fall out. What was happening was that patients would come out of the door with a prescription they didn't actually want and shove it in the hedge in disgust.

The wasted resources represented by these, and all the other ways in which patients and service users are processed in ways that don't really suit them, are a small part of what the system wastes. Some of these wasted prescriptions are there because patients were mistaken about what treatment they needed, but some are there because the doctor has not listened, or has listened but is constrained by the system. Either way, the hedge is a symbol of the waste caused by inflexibility.

*The corrosion of human-scale*

The problem with the industrialization of services is partly that it seems to go hand in hand with the idea that it should be managed from the centre by a technocratic elite. It is also part of a bundle of ideas that allows that elite to forget that human, face-to-face skills can make an impact on people's lives in a way that industrial systems just can't. Human systems are flexible and have an ability to deal with these exceptions to the rule that cost so much money in automated systems. Goodhart's Law implies that we may actually all of us be exceptions in some way or other. Human beings tend to break out of neat categories.

One London hospital carried out research in 2015 about people who go to their local Accident and Emergency Department (A&E) rather more than is comfortable. The usual definition of 'frequent attenders' is three times a year. We have heard of one patient in London who arrived by ambulance more than 200 times in one year. A surprising number of these frequent attenders are young women. They get into the habit, when they feel a bit down, of dialling 999 and spending the evening with people they trust, who they get to know and who will check them over. It hardly needs explaining that this relatively small number of patients causes a great deal of expense. It isn't that they don't need anything, but the system is currently not well organized to cope with social needs of this kind – still less to understand them.

One frequent attender in London taken up by the London Ambulance Service benefitted from a new approach that gives them a more personal, flexible kind of care, by small units, able to take them out of the system and make it work. In the case of this patient, among the successful solutions has been providing her with a cat.

There are a number of lessons here. The crucial importance of informality and flexibility when it comes to tackling rising costs. The importance of solutions at a very local, face-to-face level. The impossibility of writing a Whitehall manual on the use of cats in healthcare. But one thing above everything else: people may seem to need a great deal, but often what they need most of all is to give back – if not to people, to an animal. Give them some responsibility and it can transform their lives.

Decades ago every hospital ward in Britain carried a bottle of sherry. Elderly patients would be given a small glass before they went to bed. They were happy and they went soundly to sleep. The rise of scientific 'evidence-based medicine' meant the banishment of the bottle of sherry. There was no scientific evidence of its benefits so the NHS abolished it. Now elderly patients who have difficulty sleeping are given a sleeping tablet, at much greater expense, giving patients no pleasure and largely resulting in patients who wake up at night to visit the toilet being drowsy and often confused with consequent increased risk of accident. Once again, the technical trumped the human. Well done. Of course, nobody even considered asking the patients what they would rather have.

It should not be necessary to take people out of the system or to provide people with what they need, once and for all, if at all possible. The alternative is to maintain them in costly problems, at great expense, for the rest of their lives. Part of the problem is that the units are too big to deal with human scale problems. One of the continuing themes of public service wrong turnings is the way that the professions are often still wedded to size. It means higher salaries, more status, for a few of them – so the Whitehall tradition of economies of scale is not challenged as it should be.

In fact, what research there has been suggests that hospitals are more expensive, and schools and police forces are less effective, the bigger they are. It is true that you can imagine companies, factories, schools, hospitals or doctor's surgeries that are just too small, or rely too much on one individual. What we have to do here is to strike a balance so that institutions stay human-scale enough.

That is certainly confirmed by most research into small schools over the past generation, which has challenged the idea that schools are better when they are bigger. It is another wonderful example of the way that evidence-based policy tends paradoxically to confirm rather than challenge prejudices.

The Big Schools push began in the USA after the successful Soviet launch of the Sputnik spacecraft. American educationalists persuaded themselves that somehow only huge schools could produce enough scientists to compete with the USSR. It is one of the peculiar ways that Soviet thinking filtered into the West. The first challenge to it came from Roger Barker, describing himself as an environmental psychologist, who set up a statistical research centre in a small town in Kansas after the Second World War and researched the local schools to within an inch of their lives.

It was his 1964 book *Big School, Small School*, with his colleague Paul Gump, which revealed that – despite what you might expect – there were more activities outside the classroom in the smaller schools than there were in the bigger schools. There were more pupils involved in them in the smaller schools, between three and twenty times more in fact. He also found children were more tolerant of each other in small schools.

Most of research has been carried out in the United States, rather than the UK, but it consistently shows that small schools

(300-800 pupils at secondary level) have better results, better behaviour, less truancy and vandalism and better relationships than bigger schools. They show better achievement by pupils from ethnic minorities and from very poor families. Why should smaller schools work better? There is some consensus among researchers about this. The answer is that small schools make human relationships possible. Teachers can know pupils and vice versa.

More on schools in the next chapter. These issues interact. Services are still disconnected from each other: they are siloed, inflexible bureaucracies, too often unable to share information, share effort or to reach out upstream of ill-health or social problems and tackle the causes when they can be tackled – and when it is far more cost-effective to do so. Highly successful projects which buck the trend – from Family-Nurse Partnerships to Local Area Co-ordination – are too often side-lined and ignored by the mainstream, which seems unable to learn or change.

Hence mainstream services have so often become bureaucratic, unresponsive and ineffective, and encourage perverse incentives which encourage gaming, wasting people's time, wasting their money and wasting the capacity of the system. They are also disconnected from the people who use them (see below).

For all these reasons, budgets are still rising when the very future of public services depends on them becoming more affordable. The situation is exacerbated by the way PFI contracts and some big contractors are extracting resources from the system. We have no objection in principle to private suppliers, as long as they are accountable and responsive, but poor commissioning of big organisations, controlled by ever narrower output measures, has led to a culture of repeated, ineffective interventions – which throw costs back onto the rest of the system. The problem is not so much privatisation but gigantism, and the unfortunate tendency to commission private organisations that are only actually expert in one area – the management of target information.

In fact, all too often, the boneheaded tendency in public service privatisation has led to services being run by very large companies, insulated from competition, with extremely poor relationships with their workforce, driven by a delusion that they can control everything in detail remotely from the centre. The result, as the recent semi-collapse of rail services in the Southern rail franchise run by a subsidiary of Go Ahead, is sclerosis.

*Corroding social networks*

It is now exactly four decades since the future Nobel laureate Elinor Ostrom carried out her ground-breaking research into the systems used by the Chicago police. When she won the Nobel Prize for economics in 2009, it was doubly unusual: no woman had ever won it before, and she wasn't even an economist. She had been at Indiana University for most of her career, spending much of her time in the 1960s, by her own admission, getting her own students out of gaol after anti-Vietnam War protests.

Ostrom was fascinated by the issue of scale. When she scraped up enough money to begin research, she decided she would look at the same phenomenon which was happening across the USA of consolidating police forces into larger and larger units. She had just enough money to hire cars for her research students to drive around Indianapolis for ten days, and test out the effectiveness of different styles of policing. It was pretty clear, after the results came in, that the smaller the police force, the better they were at responding to emergency calls. It is the same in the UK, even now.

This challenged conventional thinking, which assumed then –

as it still does – that bigger is better. Her black students urged her to have a proper look at policing in Chicago, and sure enough, it was the same there. The small police forces in the black suburbs were just as effective as the huge police force covering central Chicago, which had fourteen times the funding.

The Chicago police were interested in her research and asked her why she thought the crime rate seemed to be rising when police shifted from walking the beat to driving round in patrol cars. It was here that she made her real breakthrough, understanding how much the police need the public, and how cut off they had become.

She needed a word that described that indefinable co-operation between police and public which was so easy when they walked around. She called it 'co-production'. If the police forget how much they need the public – and disappear into technocratic systems, patrol cars or bureaucracy – then crime goes up, because the public come to believe their involvement is no longer needed. It is the same pattern with doctors: they need the co-operation of patients if they are going to make them well.

This is an extension of the implications of Popper's open society and its implications are profound. Society, public services and the economy are the same in this respect: they work better if people are involved alongside professionals – not consulted (some people are not articulate enough for that; this is not about committees) but actually involved themselves as service providers, *as well as* service users.

It implies the need for a basic mutualism – and Ostrom won the Nobel prize for her work on mutualism – which binds people together in the co-production of society, and blurs the traditional boundaries between givers and receivers, between professionals and patients.

But it is more than that. Creating a more flexible public service system where human values can be brought to bear as part of their central purpose – not squeezed in by frontline staff in defiance of targets – is only part of it. Open public services are ones where the basic boundaries are blurred – between departments, between givers and receivers, producers and consumers, professionals and users. This approach means a revolution in services so that they can reach upstream of social issues and *prevent* their future workload. The cat as a solution in A&E was an example of that. Another is the way the Fire Brigade in Greater Manchester has reduced their demand by half by slowly shifting resources into preventing fires.

Rebuilding social networks is an example of this kind of prevention. It can provide some inoculation against dependence on services. It implies that service users, who are supposed to be such a deadweight on an exhausted public service system, are also assets, and miserably wasted by the current system.

The implication for the public sector is that services are not glorified assembly lines, and they are less effective and therefore more expensive when they are organised like this. They are most efficient when they are developed as hubs at the heart of a whole range of reciprocal relationships, which make possible a huge and unprecedented mobilisation of unpaid involvement by public service users, their families and their neighbours.

It also means a massive increase, not so much in volunteering because it will be outside the conventional volunteering infrastructure, but of mutual support and activity organised through the public sector. It means that every school, surgery, hospital, park or beauty spot, every beach, museum, lifeboat station, could become – as its fundamental purpose – a hub of increasing local activity. It also means that some visits to the doctor will involve questions about what you can do to help – not just about your symptoms and matching drugs, but where your passions lie and what your objectives are in life.

Of course consultation is important in running services but there has been considerable frustration that it has been so difficult. It may be that the business of asking the opinions and guidance of service users works best when they feel the kind of ownership that active involvement in delivering services alongside professionals brings.

There is no doubt also that user management or consultation is a kind of co-production, but co-production emphasises people using their *human* skills. They don't become mini-bosses when they work alongside professional staff. They are recognised for their potential to broaden and deepen services because of what they *do*, not because of what they think. It is the *doing* that's important: the co-production critique of public services, which derives from the work of Elinor Ostrom and the American civil rights lawyer Edgar Cahn denies that professionals are the only ones that do things. It is about challenging patients to play an equal role, certainly in their own health, but also in the health of those around them, and to see the same kind of co-operative relationships in every area of public services, from school children taking charge of projects in their community as part of the curriculum (see Chapter 8) to Neighbourhood Watch taking responsibility for looking out for older neighbours, as Norman Lamb proposed when he was health minister.

The whole purpose here is to change the power relationships. In fact, the ideas behind co-production suggest an answer to the problem that Beveridge wrestled with, about why services became more expensive over time: that there is something about delivering services to people who are supposed to accept them gratefully and passively – sometimes extremely passively – which undermines their ability to resist, and their willingness and ability to change, and which corrodes their ability to be heroes of their own lives.

There is also something about reciprocal services, where we ask people for something back, and give them the respect that goes with being equal partners in delivery, which can turn that situation around. It can also provide the means by which we can meet some of those urgent social needs which are so getting in the way.

**

It is a complex business setting out an agenda for public services. They look so different and so complex, and the whole system – and it is an interlocking system – works so badly together, multiplying costs. But the issue for Liberals is slightly different. It isn't whether or not the basic tasks of caring and shaping society need doing or not, or whether the state needs to take a lead. The Beveridge tradition is clear that it should. The question is whether we can be open-minded and clear-sighted enough to shift those institutions so that they work more effectively and flexibly, with frontline staff and service users working alongside each other.

The key question for Liberals is how best to construct an interlocking system that is open to challenge from below, and which is capable of learning and flexible enough to change when it does. That will mean both seeing clearly enough that the present sclerotic, centralized and inflexible system doesn't always work best for the long-term interests of the people using it now – and having a clear enough vision that we can reform it without being side-tracked. There is, in fact, no more urgent issue for Liberals as how to make public services effective, so that they actually work with a minimum of interventions, so that people can lead independent, and sometimes inter-dependent, lives. We can't any more be so bound by what our public institutions are designed to do that we blind ourselves to the fact that they don't do it very effectively.

# 8

# Emptying the classrooms

*"Imagination is more important than knowledge. For knowledge is limited to all we now know and understand, while imagination embraces the entire world, and all there ever will be to know and understand."*
**Albert Einstein**

Education has always been one of the main bastions of Liberal thought. Education was the key to liberating individuals, enabling them to be self-sufficient and make their own way in life. This is a noble aim that remains today at the heart of Liberalism everywhere. But Liberals should also recognize the limitations. In *Listen Liberal*, Thomas Frank warns: "To the liberal class, every big economic problem is really an education problem, a failure by the losers to learn the right skills and get the credentials everyone knows you'll need in the society of the future."[84]

He continues: "To the liberal class this is a fixed idea, as open to evidence-based refutation as creationism is to fundamentalists: if poor people want to stop being poor, poor people must go to college." This sort of thinking has, predictably, little resonance with the new graduate loaded with student debt who finds herself flipping burgers at McDonald's on a zero hours contract. Overall, 58.8 per cent of graduates in the UK are in jobs deemed to be non-graduate roles, according to the Chartered Institute of Personnel and Development.[85] Yes, education is important – vital even – but, for Liberals, a focus on education cannot be allowed to become an apology for the lack of a comprehensive economic policy.

Having got that out of the way, what about education?

During a recent conversation with a mother of two, she mentioned that she had recently sat down with her young teenage daughter and offered to give her any pointers and advice that she might want about relationships, sex and the like, as she was entering her adolescent years. The girl's response was simple: "Mum, anything I want to know I can find on Google." This response begs the question: what is the purpose of education in an information age?

In a recent article, columnist Simon Jenkins wrote: "There is nothing, except religion, as conservative as a school curriculum. It is drenched in archaic prejudice and vested interest."[86] Which is why it took five years of constant battle with the powers that be for a university professor friend to be allowed to design a modular curriculum that could be driven by students' own choices, rather than the usual top-down rigidity of the standard curriculum. The reality is that most education systems are struggling to keep up with the rapid transition to an information age and our fundamental approach to education remains rooted in an industrial or even pre-industrial age.

## The purpose of education

In an otherwise excellent article, columnist Peter Wilby describes the outcome of schooling as "test scores and exam results".[87] And here is exactly the problem. The purpose of our educational systems has been reduced to banal numbers – test scores and exam results. The reason – that is what is easy to measure, and bureaucrats love to measure things even if the measures used end up being, at best useless, at worst disastrous (see Chapter 7). Even if the measures used brand as failures and damage for life students with great skills, but whose aptitudes do not necessarily lend themselves to good performance in a sausage-factory educational system focused on rigid, exam-focused outcomes. Even if the obsessive focus on simplistic but measurable metrics means that schools go out of their way to exclude from admission students who may bring down their average test scores, however capable they may otherwise be.

In our view, the purpose of education for the individual is to enable him or her to make the most of their individual abilities, improve confidence and self-esteem and to be successful in their lives, success being understood broadly and self-defined. It should be the students, not the educational establishment, who choose how to define success. Education should also instill a love of learning that enables us all to seek continued learning as a lifelong pursuit – something that is vital in a rapidly changing world.

For society as a whole, education serves as one of many tools necessary to strengthen the economy overall, to narrow the gap between rich and poor, to improve social mobility, to encourage innovation and change, provide resilience, reduce dependency and provide empowerment and real participation in civic life. Though, as we have outlined above, this cannot be achieved through education alone.

Nevertheless, to us all this seems a long way from simply counting exam grades.

Andreas Schleicher, director of education and Skills at the OECD, puts it like this: "In the past, education was about imparting knowledge. Today, it is about providing students with the tools to navigate and increasingly uncertain world."[88] Our current educational systems have not yet made this transition.

The expansion in access to education over the past several decades is clearly to be welcomed. But it has also had some unintended consequences. In order to cope with the increased student volume, education has become an industrialized process, a conveyor belt that puts every student through largely identical paces, regardless of aptitude and ability. This raises one of the major issues that we face today in our societies – how do we achieve things at scale without going down the 'industrialization' route, with its consequent dehumanization. Expansion has also resulted in an elitist structure that favours academic achievement (exam results) over vocational training.

As for instilling a love of learning, in England and Wales suicide rates among students increased by 50 per cent between 2007 and 2011 despite student numbers increasing by only 14 per cent. In the USA, suicide rates among young adults aged 15-24 has tripled since the 1950s with competitiveness on test scores and the likelihood of being accepted into college being identified as significant drivers. As Zoe Williams put it in an article in the *Guardian*, schools are being turned into joyless exam factories.[89] It is hard to imagine students emerging from such an environment with a love of learning.

The cost of education also continues to soar, putting pressure on the public purse and saddling an increasing number of students with ever increasing debts – hardly the best start to life. Increasing financial pressure is yet another important contributor to the suicide rates we describe above.

And the waste. How many times have we heard people say that at least 80 per cent of what they have learned at university has proven to be of no use to them in later life?

We remember speaking to a professor who ran a photography faculty at a major university. We asked why, in a digital world, they were still teaching black and white chemical development and printing techniques. After some waffle about the importance of understanding the historical evolution of the discipline, the real reasons finally emerged. This is what they have been teaching for decades, the teachers had no skills in all the different aspects of the new digital world and the institution still had all the equipment from the analogue days.

And neither does this only apply to rapidly developing technical areas. In the UK, students had to fight the educational establishment tooth and nail to force through a broader, more appropriate approach to the teaching of economics rather than stagnant approach that had become embedded. They still have to win that battle.

## Re-thinking education

Our societies are now failing to deliver. It need not be so. Yet the failings largely persist because every so-called educational reform plan is focused on managerial and administrative matters – who should run schools, who is accountable, how do we make less money go further, should education be in private or public hands, what test scores should we be aiming for.

Such 'reforms' do not merit the name. They are merely the equivalent of re-arranging the deck chairs as the ship sinks. There has been precious little re-thinking at policy levels around the purpose of education and how best to create an educational system that is free to evolve rapidly to match the ever-changing needs of a fast moving world. Liberal politics tries to make education its own but has failed to re-think it from the ground up rather confining itself to the odd tweak here and there. Welcome though such tweaks are, they fall short of the radical spirit that should infuse Liberal politics – especially in an area such as education that is so central to Liberalism.

Tony Blair, in his autobiography *A Journey: My Political Life*, claimed that: "It's not about choice, it's about standards" – a statement that was at the time something of a mantra for David Blunkett, Blair's Secretary of State for Education.[90] They were plain wrong. Making educational policy focused on standards implies that someone, somewhere can define a set of common standards that apply to every child and young adult in the land irrespective of their individual needs, aptitudes and preferences. This is a simply ludicrous notion.

It also betrays a narrow and mistaken understanding of what one means by choice. In many systems, choice has been reduced to the ability to choose between the managerial ability of different schools to deliver to common, centrally determined standards. This is a poor definition of choice (see Chapter 7), one which reduces choice only to the ability to choose between different managerial abilities.

While having some value, this is a far too limited perspective on what choice in education should mean. It should mean the ability of parents and students to choose between fundamentally different approaches to education. It should mean the existence of schools with different philosophies, different approaches to education, different curricula and different outcomes. It should also mean flexibility even within the same school. None of this is possible if schools and universities are forced into the straitjacket of common standards measured numerically through standardized exam results.

It leads to what the educationalist Sir Ken Robinson has consistently claimed – that, through their rigidity, our schooling systems work to destroy children's creative potential.

To be sure, there are some common basics that all schools should teach – children need to learn how to read, write and add up in order to be able to function effectively in the world. And even what is meant by these basics has changed dramatically in a world of smartphones that can add up for you, check your spelling and grammar and allow you to dictate all your communications rather than write them down. But, even so, beyond the basics, a good education can take many different forms. And many of these forms have been explored for some time. From the long-standing Montessori approach to education to the more recent Luminar school system pioneered by Brazilian entrepreneur Ricardo Semler, there are now many different educational models that schools can explore.

In the Luminar system, children are not put through classes in standard subjects, rather they are presented with real world challenges to solve. Students may go through a six-month project focused on how to build a bicycle. As Semler says, you can't build a bicycle unless you have a good understanding of geometry, physics and engineering principles as well as creative design skills. Yet these skills are much more productively, and much more interestingly, taught in the context of a practical project rather than in the standard sit and listen classroom format that we all had to suffer through and that bores many students to tears.

A bicycle project also requires children to learn about the teamwork, the generation and exchange of ideas and about the practical trade-offs that always have to be made in any aspect of life. This prepares students much better for the real world and the world of work than does the classroom format. Similarly, Luminar engages students in a module focused on how we express ourselves. This includes art, dance and many other forms of expression. But it also includes writing, grammar and languages as key components of personal expression. Students engaged in these approaches understand the importance of clarity and effectiveness in modes of expression. They also understand that one can express oneself in many different ways and the value of doing so, but they also learn that, whichever ways they might choose according to their own particular aptitudes, expressing oneself has to be effective.

This kind of approach also addresses one of the most common complaints among employers – that students emerge from the educational system woefully unprepared for the world of work and especially lacking in the all important soft skills of team work, communication, practical delivery and interpersonal skills. Several years ago, we asked a friend why he had chosen to study electronic engineering at university. He said that he was interested in how to build things and wanted to learn, for example, how to build a radio. "After three years at university, my mind had been filled with complex equations that I have never ever used again. But I came out still not knowing how to build a radio."

Now, that is not to suggest that education should be limited to some kind of job training experience as some employers seem to believe. Education should be much more than that. Education should prepare youngsters to perform better in the real world. Specific job training is, and should rightly remain, the responsibility of employers – a responsibility that many employers have tried to shed in their cost cutting frenzy. But schools and universities should deliver young adults ready to learn effectively from employer job training programmes, while being able to bring their own specific input to their employers' organizations.

Employers also need to take a broader view of what they expect from the educational system. One of us used to run a consulting firm focused on a science-driven industry. We had a graduate recruitment programme and used to recruit graduates in scientific disciplines believing that they would be best prepared to be productive in our industry. One of our advisers asked why we did not also recruit graduates from the arts and the humanities. We thought he was either being facetious or hadn't grasped what we were about. But we tried it anyway.

Over time, we found that graduates in subjects that Americans collectively call the liberal arts had more open and creative minds, better skills at synthesizing information and drawing conclusions and were, in general, much better at expressing themselves and communicating both with clients and with their colleagues. They had not been beaten into non-creative submission by a scientific curriculum focused on learning 'the facts'. They had a much broader, more open-minded view of the world that was able to combine exploration and rigorous analysis with emotional intelligence and an understanding of the imperfect world of human beings.

They were much better at handling real world complexity compared to their science trained colleagues who had been trained to seek linear solutions to complex problems – and who had, in general, only been trained to approach issues from the perspective of their own individual technical discipline. And they were bright enough to learn about the scientific underpinnings of what we did in a matter of weeks.

To us, it was amazing that the same type of students going through a liberal arts education could emerge so much more rounded, with so many more skills, and were so much more valuable than those who had been through the straitjacket of a particular approach to education in science subjects. These students all started out with very similar capabilities, but emerged with a very different skill set – not because of the subjects they were interested in, but because of the approach taken to their education.

Yet, whenever there is a crunch in educational funding, it is the arts and humanities that get slashed as everyone screams that we need more engineers, more software programmers and more statisticians – in short more education in STEM subjects – if we are to thrive in the modern world. We certainly need all of that. But it's hardly all we need. None of us knows what kind of jobs will be available, and what kind of skills will be in greatest demand, when a child entering school today eventually emerges on to the job market.

What we do know, or at least believe with a fair degree of certainty, is that we will always require people who are creative, who have a broad view of the world, who have critical, analytical skills, who are able to synthesize vast amounts of information, who are comfortable with complexity and understand that linear approaches don't work in complex systems, and who are able to learn, re-learn and be flexible enough to change what they do and how they do it as the world around them changes.

None of this is achieved by an educational system still focused on transmitting knowledge. The result, as Scheicher puts it, is that: "In many economies, too many unemployed graduates co-exist with a large number of employers who cannot find workers with the skills they need."[88]

There is a stark contrast between the European and American approaches to education. The nephews of one of the authors had been brought up in educational systems in the UK and Europe before their father, a diplomat, was posted to New York. In Europe, they had done well. They were perfectly suited to the style of education and had always passed their exams with flying colours. When they moved to the USA, they experienced a dreadful shock. Their skills at learning 'the facts' were not valued. Rather they were expected to learn to gather information, synthesize, explore and then form and express their own opinions cogently and forcefully, rather than just regurgitating what they had learned. They were utterly unprepared for that and their grades dropped dramatically. Their initial reaction, naturally, was that the American system stank. Only later did they come to see its value.

The irony is that many teachers and others in the educational world understand all this and a significant proportion are doing their level best to move in new directions. But they are hemmed in, and their ideas and initiatives, are squashed by a system that is increasingly centralized and burdened by measurement and incentive systems designed to show that bureaucratic targets are being met. The closer one gets to the coalface and speaks to those involved in actual delivery, the greater the level of dissatisfaction with the direction of travel and the desire to try alternative approaches. Yet, at policy making and management levels, the focus remains on standardization and management by numbers.

Another anecdote will serve to show what Sir Ken Robinson describes as the crushing of children's creativity by the schooling system. A bright, creative thirteen-year-old was taken by his mother for an afternoon of fun where an artist would share her experience of producing art. He went where his creativity led him with the artist guiding him on use of materials. He produced some amazing stuff – better than his mother's. He loved it. His comment: "I can't so this at school because they force me to do everything their way and they tell me that what I'm doing is wrong." It beggars belief.

## Re-tooling the system

What will it take to re-tool our educational system for the needs of the twenty-first century?

*Pluralism and co-operation*

We would start by making a statement that is the inverse of the Blair-Blunkett position. It is all about choice not about standards.

As we have suggested above, a variety of schools with different approaches for education will allow parents and children to select the schools that best fit the skills, aptitudes and ambitions of the individual. Local authorities – or whoever ends up with state responsibility for education after the present UK government – should focus their attention, not on micro-managing individual schools, but on making sure that children in their area have access to various alternative approaches to education.

The provision of choice is not about improving standards simply by stimulating competition (see Chapter 7). That stems from a Market Economics 101 mindset from the 1980s. Nor is it, as the Blair government came to believe, about detailed central control. It is about encouraging the emergence of different ways of doing things so that individual children have the opportunity to flourish within whatever approach suits them. It is the way to break away from the philosophy of children as numbers to be fed into the sausage-maker and spat out at the other end, while bureaucrats with clipboards tick off measurable but largely irrelevant performance metrics.

Choice is also a means of fostering constructive collaboration rather than destructive competition. Schools that have different approaches to education are not competing with each other for the same students. Rather they are providing different products that suit different sets of students. There is therefore an opportunity for collaboration. Different schools can learn from each other and take on and adapt ideas that have sprung out of different approaches.

Teachers can also evaluate whether their particular approach best suits individual students. They may suggest that a different type of school may be more appropriate for the skills and aptitudes of some students. As Sir Michael Wilshaw, the former head of Ofsted, the UK schools regulator, put it: "A 'one-size-fits-all' model of secondary education will never deliver the range of success that [our] youngsters need."[91]

For this to work, it is necessary to reverse the trend towards centralization and management by numerical target. There is a growing consensus that the idea of testing students against a national curriculum and evaluating schools simply by exam results is a misguided and harmful approach.

"There's an obsession with Sats, which seem to be the only measure of whether a school is deemed to be successful or not," according to John Baugh, head of the highly successful independent Dragon School in Oxford.[92] His school allows children no time to pursue their own passions, to focus on their own particular skills. "Unless somehow the reins are loosened a bit to allow more space and more time, I'm afraid it will be more assessment. It's all data-based from what I can see," according to

Baugh.

It is no doubt sensible to explore the best ways to make sure that all children achieve a level of numeracy and literacy that allows them to function effectively in tomorrow's world. The age at which this should be achieved can be a subject of legitimate debate. In Germany and Scandinavia, children do not start being taught how to read until age seven. As for maths, the age at which children are able to absorb such teaching and is unlikely to be the same for every child. In general, it now seems beyond doubt that prescriptive approaches, centralized definition of standards and an incessant focus on testing from a young age all lead to more disadvantages than advantages.

They are management approaches that Frederick Taylor, with his now discredited 'scientific management' approach, would have been proud of a century ago. They are archaic and have no place in the twenty-first century. And that includes PISA league tables and all other approaches that reduce education to management by numbers.

## Oversight and regulation

If one were to move over to our vision of a pluralistic education system without uniform 'standards', how would we regulate schools and evaluate their performance?

The first thing to say about this is that to structure an educational system to serve the needs of centre is to have things exactly the wrong way up. First, we need to decide what sort of educational system we need and then we need to work out how best to evaluate and regulate.

In the pluralistic system that we are advocating, the role and approach of the regulator would be fundamentally different to what it is today. The first role would be to evaluate access. Do all children in all areas have access to a sufficiently diverse range of educational approaches that cater to all children's needs? The second role would be to encourage exchange, federation and co-operation between different schools. The school system in any area would be seen as a cluster of different skills and, like an industrial cluster, would encourage the sharing of resources so that each school could learn from the ones next door.

What about standards and performance? Here the regulators' role would be to learn from schools not to impose a top-down, standard and rigid form of evaluation and control. Schools with different approaches should, rightly, have performance measures that are different, each appropriate to what that individual school was trying to achieve. Schools would therefore be encouraged to devise their own performance measures, ones that suited their own style and their own objectives. A regulator's role would be to help schools through that process, to learn from them what might be appropriate measures and to share those insights and ideas with other schools that may have similar approaches and objectives.

Finally, the regulator would have a role in facilitating shared learning across similar schools. In this model, the role of the regulator would change from that of the finger-wagging policeman focused on inspection and box-ticking to that of a mentor, guide or counsellor – helping schools succeed in meeting their own objectives rather than in meeting one-size-fits-all standards. Failure of any schools would be considered the responsibility of the regulator as much as the responsibility of the individual school involved.

It goes without saying that such a schooling system could not possibly be run centrally by a minister and a handful of civil servants. It would require significant devolution of power and responsibility to local level. Similarly, though regulation would need to be centrally co-ordinated to benefit from knowledge gained across different places, it would also have to be structured to be close to and meet the needs of different localities. We believe that this would not only improve the outcomes of education, but it would increase motivation and enthusiasm among schools and the teaching community – something that is badly needed, because recruitment and retention of good teachers is becoming increasingly difficult.

## About teaching

The need for continued learning, changing how things are done and benefiting from the experience of others, is widely accepted in most professions. Yet it is not necessarily so in education. Teaching methods remain far behind what is possible in today's world. And a proportion, though by no means all, teachers at all levels remain wedded to their traditional ways of doing things.

In discussions with the provost at Florida International University, we were exploring different educational methods and approaches. His response was: "Yes, we'd like to do all of this but the greatest resistance will come from the faculty."

There is a potential deal to be struck, to honour the input of individual teachers – by far the major factor in the success of their pupils – in return for an acceptance that change must happen. An end to tickbox obsession with exams, in return for a new kind of teaching profession.

To be fair, resistance to change appears to be more virulent and more widespread in tertiary education than it is in primary and secondary education. But more of that later.

In our view, teaching should be a dynamic profession. Teachers, lecturers and professors at all levels should be subject to continuing education about how to improve their teaching methods. Like other professions they should have continuous accreditation – not in their subject matter (most keep up to date with that) – but in educational approaches and teaching skills. Whenever we ask children why their favourite subject is their favourite, nine times out of ten the answer is that they like the teacher and he or she generates enthusiasm for the subject. There is simply no excuse for not having continuous programmes that improve teaching skills and teaching methods.

Using data from the Education Endowment Foundation, *The Economist* found that improving teaching skills was far and away the most effective way of improving educational standards. The effects far outstripped that favourite of politicians – reducing class sizes – and at much lower cost. "All of the 20 most powerful ways to improve school-time learning identified by the study depended on what a teacher did in the classroom," they concluded. They also conclude that: "A fair chunk of what teachers (and others) believe about teaching is wrong. And ways of teaching better – often much better – can be learned."[93]

Yet the type of training teachers need is often not what they receive. Particularly in the UK, teacher training remains largely focused on academic questions rather than on practical teaching skills. Progress is also held back by the attitude of some teachers' unions which, for instance, still forbid taking notes when observing teacher performance for the purpose of giving feedback and looking towards improvement.

Yes, good teachers are not just born, they can be made. But they can only be made using the right methods – about which considerable research now exists. And good teaching cannot then be destroyed by making them work to poor performance metrics. The reality is that most 'poor teachers' can improve their skills if only they had access to the right training and continuous feedback and improvement. But we must also be realistic. There comes a point when poor teaching has to be confronted for the sake of their children. Some will not be suited to the profession and will not become good teachers. That still needs tackling. Poor teachers can be mentored and supported but, in the end, they must be helped into a different profession – just like in any other organization people whose skills and aptitudes are better used elsewhere should move there – for their own well-being and success as well as for the sake of others.

The teaching profession should also be mobile. Companies routinely rotate their staff between departments and locations to help them build skills and perspectives. This should happen with teachers too. They should have the opportunity, indeed the obligation, to move across different teaching establishments, different geographies and schools with different philosophies in order to gain different perspectives, to learn from others and continually improve their skills.

Similarly, educational establishments must start to welcome the opportunities offered by e-learning. If well incorporated into the system, it can enhance opportunity, increase student interest and bring to every single school and university the best that is available anywhere in the world. Yet, all too often e-learning is seen as a threat to teaching jobs or as something that diminishes the authority of the teacher. None of this is true. True, e-learning will require the development of new skills to make it work optimally, but there is nothing to stop those skills being developed. Quite the reverse: the face-to-face human element is absolutely critical in online teaching. It is just that it is used differently.

Finally, is it time to roll back the classroom model of teaching? One of us remains cross that, in the seven years in which he learned French the traditional way, a couple of times a week, he never really mastered the language. Yet think of the savings in resources if he had been immersed in French culture for a month.

We mentioned previously the fledgling attempts to bring business people into the classroom. But we need to go a great deal further. We need to develop ways to take pupils out of the stifling atmosphere of the classroom and into the real world. We asked Mario, a thirteen-year-old, how he would run his school if he were in charge. His response was that maths would be more interesting and more easily understandable if pupils were taken out to set up market stalls where they could sell stuff and then would have to calculate prices, how much change to give and so forth.

He also suggested that he would set up a rotation of pupils to work in different parts of the school for some time – some in the cafeteria, others in finance and administration and so on. "It would be so much more fun and we would learn more," he said. As we said in Chapter 7, those who benefit from services often know how best to run them, and are interested in working alongside professionals to do so, whatever their age.

We should aim for a world where classrooms and schools are empty most of the time because the students are out learning about life, and being made to feel confident that they can live it. Of course, this would make the running of schools more complicated. But we should ask ourselves, is the organization of schools around the classroom primarily designed to deliver the best education or is it simply the most convenient way for schools to organize themselves? The argument used in some of the rigid large schools now is that this is about teaching discipline and self-discipline. If so, it is hardly surprising that girls tend to respond better at an age when boys are that less pre-disposed to sitting still.

## Tertiary education

There may be nothing quite as conservative and resistant to change as tertiary education. We believe that the educational needs of our future depend on a total re-think of the approach to tertiary education. Here we focus on five specific aspects.

### Vocational training

Many countries such as the UK have developed an elitist educational structure that puts traditional academic education on a pedestal while disdaining vocational training and apprenticeship structures. This is not the case in other countries such as Germany and the results are obvious when it comes to the strength and resilience of the economy. Nothing holds back an economy as much as the classic snobbish attitude to education – that all attention, resources and praise should be heaped on academic education while, despite the rhetoric, vocational skills have been swept under the carpet.

In many countries, the revival of vocational education has only just started. But, even in the UK where this is all in its infancy, it has been so successful that more young people applied for apprentices at BAe systems and Rolls-Royce in 2014 than applied to Oxford and Cambridge – though that also flags up the desperate need for more, improved opportunities.

There is a long way to go before most countries have the kinds of networks of medium-sized businesses, and the training institutions that support them, that have been such a feature of life in Germany. Such an infrastructure cannot be developed without deep integration between schools, tertiary education establishments and businesses themselves. Yet, in most countries, these all seem to live in a different planet, each protecting their own patch and suspicious, and often disdainful, of the other to the detriment of all. Educational establishments need to open up to businesses and others and create integrated co-operation focused on vocational skills. Businesses, on the other hand, need to be prepared to invest time, effort and money in working with educational establishments to help them tool up so that they are able to turn out skilled, employable and productive individuals. Neither can do it on their own and neither can afford to take the view that it is solely the other's responsibility.

While we include vocational training here as part of tertiary education, preparation for it must start in the schools. First, schools must prepare pupils for a vocational tertiary education and not imbue students with a belief system that such an outcome is only second or third best – only for students who don't have the ability to go on to an academic education at university.

Secondly, integration between what goes on at school and what goes on in the outside world needs to improve dramatically. There is, in many places, already a movement to bring business people into the classroom - which is a good start. But we also need to take pupils out of the stifling atmosphere of the classroom and into the real world.

Some fledgling models already exist. In the UK up to 500 businesses around the country have been partnering with local schools, in a series of relationships forged by Business in the Community as Business-Schools 'clusters', managed by a local business that brokers the relationships. It is informal and it is a good start. These sorts of initiatives need to be deepened and scaled up substantially. Government has a role to play in encouraging and maybe requiring that they happen without giving them the kiss of death by attempting to take them over and manage them centrally.

*Modular curricula*

University curricula tend to be set by faculty and students have to tick all the boxes on a set curriculum to earn their degree. This practice is outdated and irrelevant to the modern world. The faculty, just like the rest of us, has no idea what skills will be required in five or ten years' time. Curricula tend to last for years, if not decades, beyond their useful life, while rigid curricula barely cater to the varying interests and aptitudes of different students.

A more useful approach would be for universities to put together small modules to cover specific skills areas. Modules could include a mix of teaching provided by the university itself as well as e-learning provided by other universities that may have better know-how in those areas. Students can pick and choose to compile their own degree programme depending on their own particular interests and aptitudes. They can also pick specific supervisors to guide them through their chosen programme. While this may make the life of the faculty more challenging, or at least different from what they are used to, it would be more motivating for students, more likely to generate good performance as students have chosen what they are interested in, and should give students a mix of skills and know-how that they can more easily apply in the real world.

Fortunately, there is evidence that this is starting to happen.

New degrees in some universities offer students the opportunity to mix and match different subjects rather than specializing in one or two:

> "University of Surrey student Laura Richter says she chose its liberal arts and science degree because she wanted to carry on with several subjects. "I liked psychology, languages and humanities, and I didn't want to choose one and then find two years down the line it wasn't for me," she says. "Everyone gets together from the different modules, and we bring our different skills and approaches to problems and scenarios." Her main subjects are psychology and modern languages."[94]

It is time this approach became the norm rather than the exception.

*Breaking down disciplinary boundaries*
We can imagine the howls of objection. But what happens if students choose modules from many varied disciplines? What kind of degree do we award them? The answer to that question is nobody cares.

Universities are still structured around individual disciplines, but the world doesn't care about individual disciplines. It cares about having a citizenship that can understand issues and find ways to improve them. Solutions never lie within individual disciplines but they require bringing together different skills and perspectives for which most students are not well prepared. The focus on individual disciplines leads to early and narrow specialization, and that does not serve the needs of today's complex and interconnected world. It leads to an educational culture where success is defined as knowing more and more about less and less. A world where the silos in which people are required to operate become deeper and deeper, narrower and narrower, and ever more cut off from the real world. The world that we all inhabit.

The partial response of most educational establishments is the idea of trans-disciplinarity. But that is not good enough – and, by and large, it doesn't work. That is because disciplines are not just about knowledge, they are about values. Contrast an anthropologist working in detail on one particular cultural perspective with a physicist working on characterizing the latest nano-particle, with an economist working on the economic implications of global financial flows. Each lives in her own world surrounded by people like themselves. They develop a world-view driven by their discipline and their peers. This is not a matter of knowledge. It becomes deeply embedded in their own personal core values and their own sense of self. And experts in any single discipline to not answer to society at large – they answer to their peers on whom reputation and advancement largely depends.

We attended a trans-disciplinary meeting some time ago, anthropologists focused on people and cultures clashed with conservation biologist focused on endangered species and both clashed with economists focused on economic development. They were all working on the same questions but each of their world views were so narrow that there was no point of communication, no common ground, no ability to work together. Their individual disciplinary perspectives became part of their identity that they would not surrender to alternative world-views.

A young post-doctoral philosopher described to us how, a couple of years before, she was hissed at twice when she took a class run by the history department and tried to join the discussion. She eventually had to discontinue taking the class because nobody would accept that a philosopher had any business participating in a history discussion.

Why does this happen? It happens because the issue of 'a discipline' is not a question of knowledge – rational, dispassionate knowledge that people accumulate by studying this or that subject. Different disciplines are not repositories of knowledge. They are complete cultures. They are different cultures in an ethnographic sense, each with their own values and their own unique moral compass. It becomes about identity and community. And the strong emotions that all of this generates. The pursuit of so-called knowledge becomes transformed into a moral battle of conflicting values. Jonathan Haidt in *The Righteous Mind* puts it like this: "Once people bind themselves into groups that share a common perspective, they become unable to see that there is any legitimacy in other perspectives."[95]

And it is this that makes trans-disciplinarity so very difficult to make work. Because it is not a question of different bits of knowledge that can work together with 'good management'. It is a question of fundamentally different values that tear people apart.

So not only does a structure around different disciplines fail to serve the needs of our complex and interconnected societies, it actually tears our societies apart. Our suggestion of modular curricula can serve to start breaking these silos down. A student interested in building houses might well benefit from modules that cover ethics, history, art, environmental science, aspects of anthropology or behavioural science, politics, business management, accounting, communication and advertising as well as some, though maybe not all, the usual subjects covered in an architecture curriculum.

Another interested in the same ultimate outcome may choose a very different mix, depending on how they see themselves and what their particular interests are. What their degree is labelled at the end of the day is largely irrelevant. At the end of the process, they will be much more useful people in our society for having the breadth of experience and perspectives that such a modular approach would provide.

And such a process also accepts that students are better judges of what they would like to learn to build the life they want than academics compiling standard curricula for all.

And this is not to say anything about the cross-disciplinary battles that plague university life everywhere. As far back as 1959, in his famous Rede Lecture titled *The Two Cultures*, C. P. Snow compared the cultures of art and science at Cambridge University as two groups "who had almost ceased to communicate at all, who in intellectual, moral and psychological climate had so little in common that instead of going from Burlington House or South Kensington to Chelsea, one might have crossed an ocean".

If anything, universities have allowed these deep cultural divisions to become worse over time. This does not serve the interests of good education and students must no longer be allowed to be imbued with the disciplinary bigotry of their teachers. Encouraging students to develop their own curricula that ignore disciplinary boundaries would be a good first step in that direction.

*Separating research from education*
In an article in the *Financial Times*, Dame Nancy Rothwell, president and vice-chancellor of the University of Manchester, put

it like this: "Research is a key factor in many students' choice of university. In part, because research quality drives reputation, but also because many students want to be taught in world-class facilities by leading scholars at the cutting edge of intellectual inquiry."[96]

We disagree.

The academic establishment has chosen to put research quality as the primary determinant of progress up the academic career ladder. Yet, apart from the continued assertions by academics such as Dame Nancy, there is no evidence that there is any correlation between research excellence and teaching excellence. As we have outlined earlier, teaching excellence comes from the honing of practical teaching skills not from immersing oneself in the library or the laboratory undertaking research. There is similarly no evidence that involvement in research, and the time that takes away from student interaction, contributes in any way to the quality of tertiary education.

Research only enhances university reputations because that is the way that academics have chosen to measure their worth — a measure that has no bearing on teaching excellence. In fact, it is possible that the research and teaching excellence are negatively correlated. It is not hard to imagine that those academics whose skills and aptitudes make them particularly good researchers do not necessarily possess the best teaching and educational skills.

It has become the fashion that one needs a Ph.D to get a university lecturer job. This underlines the fact that the priority for universities, supposedly educational establishments, is research and not teaching. A Ph.D is designed to give you the skills to undertake research and formulate conclusions. It does nothing to improve your teaching ability. There are no requirements to show or learn teaching abilities or to have a passion for teaching as a requirement to enter into university faculty.

A friend who is a professor at a Russell Group university in the UK put it to us like this: "[My university] repeatedly asserts that it values research and education equally. My experience of the financial and management approaches that it applies to research and education is that it does not."

He goes on to explain that while research is fully funded, academics are just allowed to get on with it and they are ultimately judged on the excellence of the output, that is not the case with teaching. "In teaching, however, the university administrators and lay managers do their utmost to increase student numbers while they progressively resile on the pre-agreed resource commitments. It is difficult to avoid the conclusion that whilst the prime driver for 'research' is usually quality and excellence, for teaching the prime driver is making money in the short term at any cost." He says that such behaviour is justified by the perceived need for tuition fees to cross-subsidize research – a position with which he personally disagrees.

In a similar vein, a friend used to be a professor of business strategy in Chicago. His classes were the best attended. He was a wonderful and inspiring teacher and it was standing room only in his lectures. But he had no interest in research. The university eventually fired him because he did not publish or bring in research funding.

The increasing disconnect between what it takes to deliver universities' primary mission – to teach – and what it takes for academics to advance their own careers is nothing short of outrageous. It is time that universities were stopped from stealing students' tuition fees (whoever is paying them) to subsidize research activities intended to advance academics' own careers. And all this says nothing about the time that is taken away from teaching duties by research commitments while ever-more teaching is delegated to more junior staff or Ph.D students.

Neither is research the only, or maybe even the best, way for academics to stay at the cutting edge of their subjects. Most other professions find it perfectly possible to keep up-to-date in their subject through reading and continuing education programmes without embarking on research programmes. These days, research programmes tend to be very narrowly focused, and rarely provide the breadth of perspectives that are so useful in giving students a broad based education.

None of this is to denigrate the need for research and the value that universities can bring in exploring new ground. But, as the costs of tertiary education continue to rise, the amount of funding that is diverted from teaching to research is nothing short of scandalous. In our view, research institutions and educational institutions should be separated. Academics should have the choice to make their preferred career in teaching or research and each should carry the same reputational and financial rewards.

Each can then focus on what they are good at and where their skills lie. Those whose interest is in research should not have to bother with teaching and marking papers (which they largely hate to do) while those who love teaching and are good at it should not be distracted by having to amass publications and research grants to stay in their job and contribute to their institution's ratings. Similarly funding for research and for education should be separate and governments should make explicit decisions as to how much money should go to each.

Some, including our professor friend quoted above, believes

that research does make a contribution to better teaching. That may be the case in some instances. But this is likely to be a matter of chance rather than anything else. Research excellence is not in any way judged by the contribution it makes to teaching excellence. It is judged by the accumulation of publications in highly ranked journals. While the incentive system that enhances a faculty's careers and reputations remains totally divorced from the quality of teaching that faculty provides, any benefit that flows from one to the other will remain random. Separating the two activities remains the only viable solution.

*Lifelong education*
Finally, we would like to make a point about the need to build an educational system focused on lifelong education.

In a fast changing world, everyone's skills are soon outdated. Continuous learning, re-training and making the previously retired productive in a contemporary world, are just as important as appropriate training of new generations. Yet they receive considerably less attention. It could be argued that such initiatives will yield quicker results. They will make those in work more productive and prepare us for an economy that will remain productive as the population continues to age.

Catering for this largely ignored need requires a shift in mindset by the educational establishment to consider their role as one that covers the whole population, not just the young. Educational establishments need to see themselves as providing lifelong stewardship alongside people's careers not just spitting out graduates and then moving on to the next set.

We also need a change in mindset within businesses. Too many businesses still regard mature employees as a high cost that can be reduced. Yet mature employees have valuable skills and institutional knowledge that cannot be replicated by new graduates. They are valuable people who can be re-trained, made continuously more adaptable and more productive and who can combine experience with adaptability to extend their working life. Our current educational structure is not set up for lifelong education. It is time that it becomes so.

## Education, politics and citizenship

Robert Maynard Hutchins in *The University of Utopia* put it like this: "The object of the education system, taken as whole, is not to produce hands for industry or to teach the young how to make a living. It is to produce responsible citizens."[97]

This perspective gets to the old argument about whether a functioning society is created by putting politics first, as was suggested by Aristotle, or by putting economics first as was much later proposed by John Locke. We believe that the two are indivisibly intertwined. We therefore see the purpose of education as preparing people for the totality of life – both political and economic. Sadly, our current education system does a particularly good job with neither.

We have addressed the deficiencies in the economic element earlier. Here we focus on whether our educational system is equipped to produce responsible citizens. It isn't. It is focused on producing engineers, mathematicians, linguists and those like them with each of those disciplines defined in too narrow and not particularly useful ways. Yet without an informed, engaged and responsible citizenry, no Liberal democracy is possible to sustain.

The failure of the educational system to imbue youngsters with a sense of civic and political responsibility can be gauged from the low turnout among the young in all elections. In the UK referendum on British exit from the EU, the young complained that their future was taken away from them by the votes of the elderly. Yet, they should not blame anyone but themselves. Turnout among the young was significantly lower than among the elderly.

We have mentioned earlier the educational degradation of the humanities in favour of more utilitarian subjects. Similarly, subjects like civics have all but disappeared from any curriculum while politics was never a subject of much discussion in schools. We believe that 'citizenship' should be an important part of school curricula and children should be exposed to discussion about political structures, the economy and the rights and responsibilities that go with being a good citizen.

We also suggest that Europe might take a leaf from the American educational model where any university entrant needs initially to enrol in a general foundation course that covers broad issues that are relevant to how students will eventually live in the world. That could include history, philosophy, economics, politics, our legal system and other relevant subject areas. Without building a sense of civic responsibility and encouraging civic engagement by the young, our Liberal democracies will not survive and we will fail to build the cohesive and informed society that we would all like to see.

Lying behind this is the need for schools to spread confidence and self-belief. Regions of ingrained poverty, where primary schools are known to be effective, can reasonably look to the secondary school system and wonder if it has let down generations by failing to give them the confidence they needed to live.

# 9

## Fierce Liberalism

*"I was brought up to believe that there is no virtue in conforming meekly to the dominant opinion of the moment. I was encouraged to believe that simple conformity results in stagnation for a society, and that ... progress has been largely owing to the opportunity for experimentation, the leeway given initiative, and to a gusto and a freedom for chewing over odd ideas."*
**Jane Jacobs**

Jane Jacobs was a phenomenon, born in Canada and bringing up her children in New York City. It was her experience campaigning, alongside other women of a similar age, against the titan of inner urban motorways, Robert Moses, that led to her groundbreaking book *The Death and Life of the Great American Cities*.[98] Why should we stop building, Moses is supposed to have said: the only people against us are "a bunch of mothers"?

But Jacobs won the battle. The New York bulldozer that drove through impoverished communities was put away, at least as far as urban motorways were concerned. The same thing happened in London, when the notorious Motorway Box scheme was set aside in 1975 after the Conservatives were trounced at the Greater London Council elections that year. Though the damage had been done: most of the worst urban riots – Brixton, Toxteth – six years later, took place in neighbourhoods blighted by urban motorway plans. The same is true in New Orleans where a highway split the city in two condemning one part of it to poverty and crime.

Every political tradition claims Jane Jacobs as her own. The free traders like her because of her emphasis on the small-scale and against big planning. The Greens like her because of her emphasis on fine mesh neighbourhoods and import replacement. But in her understanding that conformity is dangerous to open societies – for all the reasons Karl Popper set out – she was a Liberal, in the European definition. She was a Liberal in the English tradition because of her emphasis on life, lived at human scale by real people.

Here is her description of how small shops in Greenwich village make a hidden difference to the economy, a concept known later as 'social capital':

"One ordinary morning last winter, Bernie Jaffe and his wife Ann supervised the small children crossing at the corner; lent an umbrella to one customer and a dollar to another; took custody of two keys; took in some packages for people in the next building who were away; lectured two youngsters who asked for cigarettes; gave street directions; took custody of a watch to give the repair man across the street when he opened later; gave out information on the range of rents in the neighbourhood to an apartment seeker; listened to a tale of domestic difficulty and offered reassurance; told some rowdies they could not come in unless they behaved and then defined (and got) good behaviour; provided an incidental forum for half a dozen conversations among customers who dropped in for oddments; set aside certain newly arrived papers and magazines for regular customers who would depend on getting them; advised a mother who came for a birthday present not to get the ship-model kit because another child going to the same birthday party was giving that; and got a back copy (this was for me) of the previous day's newspaper out of the deliverer's surplus returns when he came by."[99]

That is the heart of the new Liberalism. It is about ordinary life, as it is actually lived, and about human life too. It is civilized, humane and practical, but the promotion of it also needs to be fierce. Part of the reason why Liberalism has found the transition hard in the twentieth century is that it has been difficult to disentangle Liberalism from the traditional lever of Liberalism – money – which automatically drove out privilege and aristocracy, and has done for centuries. The difficulty is that money keeps on corroding: when it comes to undermine human values and community and the underpinnings of civilization, then Liberalism has to find itself on the other side.

"There is no wealth but life," wrote John Ruskin, who explained he was emphatically not a Liberal, but the sentiment is the very heart of Liberalism.[100]

The other reason, as we have seen, that Liberalism lost its way is that it became associated with bland compromise. It grasped the centre, afraid that, as Yeats put it, it "could not hold", but forgot that it has a separate and more urgent purpose. Not that those who campaign on the centre ground have forgotten their radicalism, but that they have lost faith in it as an electoral asset and as a source of moral authority. But for it to be that, Liberalism needs to transform itself from bland, politically correct compromise, which comes across as weakness and lack of any sort of conviction, to a radical Liberalism that is fierce and uncompromising in the pursuit of its ideals.

In fact, it was UK Liberals, tiptoeing into a new radicalism in the 1960s, that were often at the forefront of campaigns like Jane Jacobs, battling high rise flats or community demolition, furious at concrete soullessness, the only political tradition that did so. And Liberals do this not because they are against progress or change. But because they are against change that can only come from dehumanization and the construction of a soulless, bureaucratic, centralized state.

Nor is it to suggest that Liberals in government have failed to achieve on behalf of their electorate. Justin Trudeau in Canada is opening up a new kind of radicalism in practice. The Lib Dems in government in the UK pressed ahead with ambitious pension reforms, with green investment, and the pupil premium to shift the in-built bias against poor children in schools. Ideas wear out, and they need to be thought through afresh, but there are signs that this is happening. It is our contention in this book that those ideas need to be an amalgam of traditional Liberalism applied in whole new ways to the world – with these three interlocking foundations:

1. A society and institutions that encourages and enables that vital challenge from below.

2. Human-scale institutions, communities, buildings, services and businesses.

3. Awareness of community but openness to the world.

**

The spectre of powerlessness is a powerful fear at the beginning of the century: not just the powerlessness of communities in the face of bureaucracy, or consumers in the face of corporate centralization, but the powerlessness of the institutions that were designed to shape our lives and which purport to rule us now. It was the sense of powerlessness that so many people shared that drove the Brexit vote in the summer of 2016.

This powerlessness is shared by rulers and ruled alike, though both collude in the pretence that everything remains the same – that benevolent institutions continue to watch over us, that professionals and politicians retain their power to act, that our democratic institutions hold our rulers to account. In fact, the sense of powerlessness is spreading corrosively through society and the political establishment. It has led to the rise of the populist right and the populist left, ultra conservative forces in both respects. It has led to a dangerous vacuum in the body politic.

This disease takes different forms in different corners of the western world, though it may be at its most acute across the Atlantic, where big money and corporate purchase has hollowed out national politics, leaving it a powerless, posturing and populist. Their place has been taken in the USA, which retains a highly devolved system of government, by the new pragmatism of the city mayors.

That option is not yet open to highly centralized Britain, where the ruling metropolitan elite clings greedily to the last illusions of control – centralizing it in Whitehall and in a dwindling number of international semi-monopolies, which have taken on the power offered them so willingly by the political elite.

In the UK, also, a deeply conservative right and a deeply conservative left, aided by a scandalous and indefensible electoral system that insulates them from the concerns of their voters, are condemned to fight and refight the old political battles of the twentieth century – how much of GDP should be public and how much private, *laissez-faire* versus state control, for or against 'business'. Party elites batter the same old language, shorn of meaning, and the same old political rituals, dressing themselves in the uniforms of long-forgotten disputes – long since resolved in most of the world. The result is a political elite that prefers symbolic gestures to genuine action, prefers minor kerfuffles about regulatory tweaks to the wholesale reforms that are so badly needed, and prefers imperial, numerical control to human flexibility.

Nor is the political world any longer prepared to use what power it still has to make the changes we need for this new century, already in its teenage years. It is depressing and it is alienating, and it allows a dangerous cynicism to undermine the shared culture of Britain and Europe. No wonder people feel alienated and cynical.

It also leads to a core irony. We live in a period of unprecedented new thinking, an exciting era of fizzing ideas, practical ones, in every area of public life – some using new technologies; more involving social innovation that shapes the institutions of the future. The only place where these ideas and debates do not penetrate is into the political establishment, for whom the business of government means the study and the manipulation of nudges, prods and signals to herd the great British population this way and that, according to the will of the great bureaucracies of state.

That is the background to the birth of a new, fiercer Liberalism, designed to tackle this sense of powerlessness head on. It exists in the political territory mapped out in the USA and described as the 'radical centre'. This is centrist in the sense that it rejects the conventional right and the conventional left. It is centrist in the sense that it denies that the real issues are expressable in those terms. It is emphatically *not* centrist in the sense of compromise between the deadeningly conventional issues, or by eking out a middle path as lowest common denominator (the Third Way was not radical, but represented a capitulation to the existing power structures). It denies that the conventional issues of right and left need compromise; quite the reverse, it suggests that they are aspects of each other. It is radical in the sense that – beyond the great gulf of our seats of government, where the governing classes operate in their powerless bubbles – it tries to look clearly and unflinchingly at the world as it really is. It sees our exhausted institutions, not through the lenses of what they ought to be, but for what they actually are.

It is also emphatically ranged against the only other political ideology left standing after Brexit: nationalism, with its narrow truths, its blindness and its intolerance. But nationalism can't govern effectively. It lacks the Liberal commitment to learning from the challenge from below. Liberalism can learn and make things happen; nationalism can't.

Of course, the 'radical centre' is hardly a new idea. It has been traced in the USA back to the pragmatism of Benjamin Franklin and the radical determination of Theodore Roosevelt. In the UK, it reflects the uncategorizable radicalism of Cobbett, Popper or Grimond. It is about seeing clearly. "Hopefully one day soon the question will be: how much can you synthesize, how much do you dare to take it all in?" wrote the US commentator Mark Satin in his book *Radical Middle*.[101]

As it does in Europe, the Radical Centre in the USA argues that open societies think more effectively, and more pragmatically, than closed ones – that societies founded on human-scale values learn faster and more tolerantly than bureaucratic ones, or virtual ones, or rationalized ones.

There is the same agenda, and it is an urgent one. And the first task, and the most difficult one, is to hammer out a practical, achievable agenda to tackle the huge disruption to the economy and people's lives that seems to be coming over the next generation, thanks to the automation of most jobs by IT and the centralized, monopolistic ownership of most of the benefits. And in the UK from the profound rejection of globalization. That is the urgent task which destiny has assigned to the Radical Centre and to Liberal thinkers and do-ers worldwide.

**

The Austrian writer Stefan Zweig was at the pinnacle of fame and success when the rise of Hitler forced him into exile. He eventually killed himself in despair at the future of the world, and of Europe in particular, in 1942. He has written in his autobiography *The World of Yesterday,* something of the sense of Europe that spread across our continent during his youth:

"When Bleriot made the first cross-Channel flight in an
aeroplane, we rejoiced in Vienna as if he were a hero of our own
nation; pride in the triumphs of our technology and science,
which succeeded one another by the hour, had led for the first
time to a European sense of community, the development of a
European identity. How pointless, we said to ourselves,
frontiers were if it was child's play for any aircraft to cross them,

how provincial and artificial were customs barriers and border guards, how contrary to the spirit of our times that clearly wished for closer links and international fraternity!"[102]

Zweig was writing about the period of the last years of peace before the First World War, and he recognized the irony: "Perhaps, ungrateful as human beings are, we did not realize at the time how strongly and securely the wave bore us up. But only those who knew that time of confidence in the world knew that everything since has been regression and gloom".

Of course, that sense of a European culture was hardly new either. It goes back to the pan-European Roman Catholic culture of the middle ages. In fact, England has railed against the confines of Rome long before it chafed at the ties of Brussels. Liberals have been in the forefront of the attempt to rebuild that continental sense of shared culture and achievement, and especially perhaps in the UK which has always been so ambivalent about its involvement with continental Europe.

So it was that it was the previously mentioned Liberal, Noel Newsome, who led the pan-European broadcasting from London in the Second World War, and whose plan for a continental radio station based in Radio Luxembourg, to build on what wireless links had managed in more than 30 languages every day, was vetoed by the UK government in 1945.[103] So it was that it was the Liberal leader Jeremy Thorpe whose support for joining the then European Economic Community made it politically possible for Edward Heath to take the UK into membership in 1973.

David Cameron was ridiculed when he described the threat of a European war – albeit maybe war fought by different means to the conventional – if the UK was to leave the European Union. But the testimony of Stefan Zweig is enough to show that he was right – and just how far the ambitions and frustrations across that continent can tear them apart. It happened twice over the past century, after all, and when the lamps go out in Europe – to coin a Liberal phrase from Sir Edward Grey – they plunge the whole world into darkness.

But we have to be honest, as we described in the last chapter. The threat to that common sense of European culture, that can lift humanity up just as it can tear humanity down when it goes wrong, doesn't just come from the racists and xenophobes. It comes from conservatives who don't understand the dangers of unlimitedly rootless populations, who kowtow to the powers of bankers and debtors, and it comes from Liberals who ushered fascism back into Europe by their adoption of a disastrous and illiberal single financial system and currency. It comes as much from the Europhiles as it does from the Europhobes.

But these threats simply underline the urgency that Liberalism renews itself, understands what is at stake and their responsibility in Europe, the crucible of human futures and the birthplace and source of Liberalism. They have to rediscover their drive, their practical thinking, their ability to see beyond the importance of existing institutions, and most of all, they need to relight the fierce fire that allowed Liberalism to shape Europe in generations gone by.

## Notes

[1] Rabinow, Paul (2007), *Marking Time: On The Anthropology of the Contemporary,* Princeton: Princeton University Press.

[2] Laws, David and Marshall, Paul (2004), *The Orange Book: Reclaiming Liberalism,* London: Profile.

[3] Gottfried, Paul (2001), *After Liberalism: Mass Democracy in the Managerial State,* 2nd edtn, Princeton: Princeton University Press.

[4] Kaletsky, Anatole (2010), *Capitalism 4.0: The Birth of a New Economy,* London: Bloomsbury.

[5] https://www.project-syndicate.org/commentary/economic-development-requires-effective-governments-by-angus-deaton

[6] Starr, Paul (2007), *Freedom's Power: The True Force of Liberalism,* New York: Perseus.

[7] Gottfried (2001), *op cit.*

[8] Wilentz, Sean (2005) *The Rise of American Democracy: Jefferson to Lincoln,* W. W. Norton, New York.Quoted in Edwards, Mickey (2012). *The Parties Versus The People: How to Turn Republicans and Democrats into Americans.* Yale University Press. Kindle Edition. (178)

[9] John Lubbock (2012), *Prehistoric Times: As Illustrated by Ancient Remains and the Manners and Customs of Savages,* New edition, Charleston: Nabu Press.

[10] G. K. Chesterton (2008), *Orthodoxy,* New edition, Charleston: Nabu Press, 49.

[11] Belloc, Hilaire (1912), *The Servile State,* London: Foulis.

[12] Fulford, R (1959) *The Liberal Case*, Penguin, Harmondsworth, 79.

[13] Orwell, George (1937), *The Road to Wigan Pier*, London: Victor Gollancz,195.

[14] Tuchman, Barbara W (1984). *The March of Folly: From Troy to Vietnam*. Kindle Edition 2014. Random House Trade Paperbacks, New York. Location 7332

[15] http://history.hanover.edu/courses/excerpts/163locke.html

[16] http://plato.stanford.edu/entries/enlightenment/

[17] Johnson, Paul (1997), *A History of the American People*, London: Orion.

[18] Žižek, Slavoj (2009), *First as Tragedy, Then as Farce*, London: Verso.

[19] Swift, Jonathan (1726), *Gulliver's Travels Into Several Remote Regions of the World*. DC Heath & Co Publishers, 1900. Kindle Edition. 737

[20] Crouch, Colin (2004), *Post-Democracy*, Bristol, Polity Press.

[21] Naim, Moises (2013), *The End of Power*, New York: Basic Books.

[22] Deaton, Angus (2015), 'Statistical objectivity is a cloak spun from political yarn,' *Financial Times,* Nov 2.

[23] Frank, Thomas (2016) *Listen Liberal: Or Whatever Happened to the Party of the People*. Metropolitan Books. Kindle Edition, 390

[24] http://www.demos.co.uk/files/multipleidentities.pdf

[25] https://philosophynow.org/issues/58/The_Death_of_Postmoderni sm_And_Beyond

[26] http://davidboyle.blogspot.co.uk/2011/06/longing-for-authenticity.html

27 Helminiak, Daniel (1973), *The Human Core of Spirituality*, New York: SUNY Press.

28 https://hbr.org/2014/08/case-study-do-business-and-politics-mix

29 Boyle, David and Zammit-Lucia, Joe (2015), *A Radical Politics for Business*, Steyning: New Weather Institute/WOLFoundation.

30 Westen, Drew (2007), *The Political Brian: The Role of Emotion in Deciding the Fate of the Nation*. Public Affairs. Kindle Edition. 4701

31 http://www.panarchy.org/keynes/national.1933.html

32 Laws, David (2016).*Coalition*, Biteback Publishing. Kindle Edition. Location 6525

33 Legrain, Philippe (2014) *European Spring: Why Our Economies and Politics Are In A Mess – And How To Put Them Right*. CB Books

34 Stiglitz, Joseph (2016). *A split euro is the solution for the single currency*. Financial Times, August 17, 2016. Accessed online.

35 Tuchman, Barbara W. (2011). *The March of Folly: From Troy to Vietnam*. Random House Publishing Group. Kindle Edition.(Kindle Locations 222-226)

36 Fishwick, Carmen and Guardian Readers (2016), 'Meet 10 Britons who voted to leave the EU'. *Guardian*, 25 Jun. Accessed online.

37 Boyle, David (2016) *V for Victory*, Steyning: The Real Press.

38http://www.neweconomics.org/blog/entry/scotpound-a-new-digital-currency-for-scotland

39Lietaer, Bernard and Belgim, Stephen M. (2004), *Of Human Wealth: Beyond greed and scarcity*, Boulder.

40 See for example Boyle, David (2011), *More than Money*, London NESTA.

[41] Boyle, David (2014), *The Potential of Time Banks to support Social Inclusion and Employability,* Seville: European Commission.

[42]http://www.panarchy.org/keynes/national.1933.html

[43]http://www.theguardian.com/media/2014/jul/06/matthias-dopfner-fight-google

[44] Mason, Paul (2015), *Postcapitalism,* London: Penguin.

[45] Boyle, David (2016), *Prosperity Parade,* Steyning: New Weather Institute.

[46] Rifkin, Jeremy (2014), *The Zero Marginal Cost Society,* New York: Palgrave Macmillan.

[47] Sauga, Michael (2014), 'The Zombie System: How Capitalism Has Gone Off the Rails', *Der Speigel,* 23 Oct.

[48] Quoted in Sauga (2014), op cit.

[49] Boyle, David (2014), *Broke: How to Survive the Middle Class Crisis,* London: Fourth Estate.

[50] From Sauga (2014), op cit.

[51] Kaletsky, Anatole (2010), *Capitalism 4.0: The birth of a new economy,* London: Bloomsbury.

[52] See more on this in Boyle (2014), op cit.

[53] Quoted in Cassidy, John 'What good is Wall Street?', *New Yorker,* 29 Nov. 2010.

[54] Kaletsky (2010), op cit.

[55] See for example Boyle, David and Greenham, Tony (2015) *People Powered Prosperity,* Steyning: New Weather Institute.

⁵⁶ Glaeser, E.L. and Kerr, W. (2010), 'The Secret to Job Growth: Think Small', *Harvard Business Review*, July.

⁵⁷ Fleming, D.A. and Goetz, S.J. (2011), 'Does Local Firm Ownership Matter?', *Economic Development Quarterly*, August, vol. 25, (3), 277-281.

⁵⁸ Lord Sharkey (2013), Speech in Hansard, House of Lords, 15 Oct.

⁵⁹ See for example: Hakenes, H., Schmidt, R. and and Xie, R. (2009), 'Public banks and regional development: evidence from German savings banks'.

⁶⁰ European Association of Co-operative Banks (2010), Latest key figures on the sector, retrieved from http://www.eacb.eu/en/cooperative_banks/key_figures/last_key_fig ures.html

⁶¹ See Zammit-Lucia, Joe et al (2016), *Quantitative Easing: The debate which never happened*, London: Radix.

⁶² The 2015 survey of entrepreneurs across Europe found that the main motivation of 43 per cent of them was to "make a difference".

⁶³ Poli, Corrado (2015*), Environmental Politics. New Geographical and Social Constituencies,* New York: Springer.

⁶⁴ http://www.nytimes.com/2016/03/13/opinion/sunday/the-global-solution-to-extinction.html?_r=0

⁶⁵ Poli (2015), *ibid.*

⁶⁶ Scharmer, Otto and Kaufer, Katrin (2013), *Leading from the Emerging Future: From Ego-System to Eco-System Economies*, New York: Berrett-Koehler.

⁶⁷ Boyle and Zammit-Lucia (2015), *op cit.*

[68] Haque, U. (2013), *The New Capitalist Manifesto: Building a Disruptively Better Business*, Cambridge: Harvard Business School Press.

[69] http://www.commonland.com/en/4returns

[70] http://eu.patagonia.com/enPL/patagonia.go?assetid=9182

[71] www.unepinquiry.org

[72] New York State Energy Planning Board (2014) *Shaping the Future of Energy*. New York State Energy Plan. Volume 1. 2014 Draft

[73] Young, Michael and Willmott, Peter (1957), *Family & Kinship in East London*. Humanities press Intl.

[74] Beveridge, William (1942), *The Report of the Inter-Departmental Committee on Social Insurance and Allied Services*, London, HMSO.

[75] Beveridge, William (1948), *Voluntary Action: A Report on Methods of Social Advance*, London, Allen & Unwin.

[76] Quoted in Participle (2008), *Beveridge 4.0*, London.

[77] http://www.vahs.org.uk/wp-content/uploads/2011/04/Bernard-Harris-paper.pdf

[78] Blond, Phillip (2010), *Red Tory: How Left and Right have broken Britain*, Faber & Faber, London, 282.

[79] See for example Seddon, John (2014), *The Whitehall Effect,* Axminster: Triarchy Press.

[80] Seddon (2014) *ibid.*

[81] Boyle, David (2013), *Barriers to choice - a review of public services and the government's response*, London: Cabinet Office. https://www.gov.uk/government/publications/barriers-to-choice-public-services-review [Accessed 9 August 2013]

82 Wood, C. (2010), *Personal Best*, Demos, London.

83 Ralph Broad (2012), *Local Area Co-ordination*, London: Centre for Welfare Reform.

84 Frank, Thomas (2016). *Listen, Liberal: Or, What Ever Happened to the Party of the People?*. Henry Holt and Co.. Kindle Edition, 20.

85 http://www.bbc.com/news/education-33983048

86 Jenkins, Simon (2016). *'Our fixation with maths doesn't add up.' Guardian*, 10 March. Accessed online.

87 Wilby, Peter (2016), 'Parents out, chief executives in: our schools will be anything but free'. *The Guardian*, 21 March. Accessed online.

88 Schleicher, Andreas (2015), *Education in an Uncertain World*. Project Syndicate, December 16. https://www.project-syndicate.org/commentary/education-technological-skills-more-important-by-andreas-schleicher-2015-12

89 Williams, Zoe (2016), 'Do we want our children taught by humans or algorithms?' *Guardian*. 1 May. Accessed online https://www.theguardian.com/commentisfree/2016/may/01/humans-algorithms-children-nicky-morgan-school-boycott

90 Blair, Tony (2010). *A Journey: My Political Life*. Vintage; Reprint Edition

91 Weale, Sally (2016). 'One size fits all' system lets down less academic pupils, warns Ofsted chief. *Guardian*, 18 Jan. Accessed online.

92 Weale, Sally (2016). 'State schools too 'under the cosh' to match our success – Dragon school head.' *Guardian* 31 Mar. Accessed online.

93 Teaching the Teachers. *The Economist*, June 11, 2016.

94 Lightfoot, Liz (2016). 'Universities enter brave new world with mix 'n' match courses'. *Guardian,* 16 Aug. Accessed online.

[95] Haidt, Jonathan (2012). *The Righteous Mind: Why Good People Are Divided By Politics and Religion.* Vintage. Kindle Edition.

[96] http://www.ft.com/cms/s/0/c56ee05e-0301-11e6-99cb-83242733f755.html#axzz4Co4qaYOi

[97] Hutchins, Robert Maynard (1953), *University of Utopia*, Chicago: University of Chicago Press.

[98] Jacobs, Jane (1993), *The Death and Life of the Great American Cities,* New edition, London: Vintage.

[99] Jacobs (1993), *ibid.*

[100] Ruskin, John (1985), *Unto This Last and Other Writings*, London: Penguin (first edition published 1861).

[101] Satin, Mark (2009), *Radical Middle: The politics we need now*, New York: Basic Books.

[102] Zweig, Stefan (1942), *The World of Yesterday*, London: Pushkin Press.

[103] Boyle, David (2016), *V for Victory*, Steyning: The Real Press.

## About the publishers

Radix is a think tank for the radical centre of contemporary politics. Our aim is to re-imagine the way government, institutions and society function based on open source participative citizenship.

We believe that the framing of politics as right *versus* left belongs to a bygone age. It leads to limited perspectives and political paralysis. We live in an exciting era fizzing with ideas, dynamism and human potential. Capturing this energy and converting it to political action can only be achieved by engaging with a radical centrism that is bold and that rejects viewing every issue from the limited perspectives of right and left – both inherently conservative forces.

Radix is a bold project to kick-start the thinking that is needed for politics to embrace technology, innovation, social and cultural change. We explore approaches that can harness the creativity of our time. Our areas of focus are the political economy, enterprise, technology and finance. We believe that these areas offer the greatest potential for positive change.

*Find out more:* **www.radix.org.uk**